The Art
of Getting People to
Say
Yes

SIX STEPS TO EFFECTIVE PERSUASION SKILLS (EPS)

The Art
of Getting People to
Say ✓
Yes

SIX STEPS TO EFFECTIVE PERSUASION SKILLS (EPS)

ARVINDER S. BRARA
INTERNATIONAL MANAGEMENT CONSULTANT
&
Co-author of PRACTICAL GUIDE TO MANAGING PEOPLE
along with Eugene Richman

A WVPD ORIGINAL

Books from Wisdom Village (Publications Division) envision to enhance and enrich its readers with life changing experiences from the mind, body and soul genres. They strive towards holistic development.

Editorial & Production   Charushilla Narula

ISBN 978-81-906555-7-6

Published by: Available at:

indiatimes
W V P D Wisdom Village (Publication Division)   Shopping
Knowledge is information. Wisdom is transformation.

WVPD is a part of Wisdom Village
164, Aravali Apartments,
Alaknanda,
New Delhi – 110019

To Book Your Orders:
Log onto: www.shopping.indiatimes.com
Email: wisdomvillageindia@gmail.com
Or Call: +91 98115 14287

Printed by : J. K . Offset & Packaging, C-21, DDA Sheds, Okhla, Phase-I, New Delhi-20

TABLE OF CONTENTS

Referring serious difficulties to helpful experts
Adapting problem people to group objectives
Changing problem people into assets

ACKNOWLEDGEMENTS

First and foremost my thanks are due to the late Peter Drucker, the world's most respected management guru of all time. When I sought his advice before starting work on this book, he gave me invaluable words of encouragement and guidance which I will cherish for ever.

I have to also thank C. K. Prahlad who has always encouraged and inspired me to present fresh thinking and a bold new approach to making people more adept.

Deciding on a suitable title of the book is very important and my thanks are due for this to my dear friend from East West Center, Hawaii days, Neil Abercrombie (US Congressman from Hawaii) and Harish Amar, erstwhile Dean of West Coast University.

Kamal Meattle has always encouraged new ideas and I thank him for writing the foreword for this book.

Pavan Choudary, the bright light of Wisdom in an emerging India, needs special thanks for his spontaneous encouragement and help in publishing this book.

Thanks are also due to the following:

Charushilla Narula for being an excellent editor who painstakingly went through every line of the book with tremendous insight to improve it considerably.

My secretary, M. K. Bhattacharya who despite his onerous duties took out time to work on this book's initial drafts with great enthusiasm.

To Wisdom Village, for the wisdom to identify useful books like this one and to publish them with excellence.

To clients of Mantec Consultants Pvt. Ltd., who encouraged the publication of this book, partly because their own employees could become more effective from reading it.

To IIT Delhi, Center for Systems and Management Studies and IIM Calcutta where I have been visiting faculty in the past, for feeding my love to share my experiences and skills with a broader audience of top management personnel, practicing executives and students.

To my father Brig. (Dr.) Narindar Singh Brara, wife Dolly Brara and son Ishwinder Brara for adjusting to my schedules and providing unstinting support. To them go my heartfelt appreciation and special thanks.

ARVINDER S. BRARA

FOREWORD

We interact with people everyday, in business or at home.

I am convinced that this book will help us understand others and be aware of the skills necessary for getting our point of view accepted. To get a 'YES' even though the answer would otherwise, have been a 'NO'.

The author has coined the acronym: 'OPOS PC' – pronounced, 'Ooh Pos Pee Cee' that should serve us as a memory aid to learn the art of opening a conversation, probing, objection handling, supporting, proving and closing.

The book provides insights of practical behavior to help people understand how to deal with people with regards to understanding of each others needs, wants, hopes, desires and aspirations.

It also shows how to effectively initiate change required for delivering acceptable results.

This book is a worthwhile read for all who want to improve their ability to effectively deal with others.

Kamal Meattle
CEO, Paharpur Business Centre
Former Member, Board of Governors, IIT Delhi

Chapter 1

INTRODUCTION
Everyone Persuades Many Times A Day

In this world due to social, family and business issues you have to deal ceaselessly with different kinds of people. Therefore, learning how to motivate and persuade people to say, "YES", or getting them on your side, is the most important skill you can use in your day to day interactions. This book is aimed at providing you with an insight into the behaviour of people around you and helping you learn how you can motivate people to accept your ideas to accomplish your personal and organizational objectives.

My motivation in writing this book is to help managers, sales personnel, business executives, professionals and individuals in all walks of life to get their ideas accepted in their day to day interactions, for improving their inter personnel relationships and overall effectiveness. We are often discouraged when our bosses or juniors do not agree with our views even when it is logical to do so. Reading this book will help you develop skills to change the course of sales pitches, superior-subordinate relationships and your personal relationships too. You will master the art of getting a "Yes" in a very agreeable manner, even from people who have said a firm "No".

The book is the key to develop practical skills for effective persuasion leading to success and desired results, quickly and easily, in whatever vocation one pursues. Every person can develop behavioural skills by reading this book to better control human responses and reactions. Each chapter of the book deals with a specific skill. This is a useful feature as it enables the reader to learn these skills one by one and ultimately use all the skills to become more effective in day-to-day interactions.

The only qualification required to learn effective persuasion skills (EPS) is a real desire to do so. These skills are a result of in-depth analysis of human behaviour that is predictable and lends itself to scientific study. It is a simple but very powerful body of knowledge, which can help bring greater achievements, happiness and understanding in everyday living.

It is interesting to note that all of us are involved everyday in convincing others about our point of view. This includes communicating to get acceptance of ideas, thoughts or concepts. These are persuasion requiring situations in the broader sense. Persuasion is not restricted to professional sales people only. In fact every individual is in a persuasion demanding situation many times a day - whether an executive, housewife, student, teacher, salesman, managing director, government official or any one for that matter. So skills to get people on your side are not only required by the persons involved in pushing a product or service but by everyone. Effective Persuasion Skills (EPS) can benefit all of us . These skills are imperative to get a commitment from others to help achieve our objectives.

Moreover, with increasing competition today, it becomes important to help improve individual capabilities. You can become many times more effective in your individual capacity by learning effective persuasion skills. When you consult various sections of the book repeatedly, you will be able to absorb these skills more and more completely. The following real life example of someone who I have trained will help to illustrate the usefulness of Effective Persuasion Skills (EPS) in everyday situations:

An ex-airforce officer, Suresh (real name withheld) after pre-mature retirement took up a job with a consulting company but was not doing well. To add to that, he was very worried about his son who was not good in his studies. He openly expressed anxiety about his future. His family became rather disjointed and tension loomed at most occasions. Suresh got an opportunity to be exposed to the concept of "Effective Persuasion Skills" and really got excited about using it to help him in his life. He used these persuasion skills to help convince his son to improve himself, start studying and producing results. He had learnt that to persuade you have to probe, understand and relate to the other person and get him to think likewise. Not only did he use these skills to solve his son's problems, he also used these skills to improve his own performance on the job. He was thrilled when he was successful in getting a ready 'yes' from his people rather smoothly. Finally, he solved his family problems very effectively. Today the family members share a good rapport amongst themselves and are doing extremely well. Suresh gives credit to using "Effective Persuasion Skills" (EPS) for his success professionally and socially. His son went on to do his MBA from New York and is today a very successful professional. He also learnt effective persuasion skills from his father.

The book has uniquely brought out that Effective Persuasion Skills can be learnt through a predictive and proven model (OPOS-PC). These are 6 steps which are based on an in-depth understanding of human behaviour:

O Opening Statement
  - How you should open a conversation.
P Probing
  - How to understand the other person's needs better by probing.
O Objections Handling
  - How to convert objections to acceptance.
S Supporting
  - How to reassure and introduce supporting examples.
P Proving
  - How to prove and expand benefits of your ideas and thoughts.
C Closing
  - How to get a "Yes" through a number of proven techniques.

Tip:
To easily remember the model 'OPOS-PC' pronounce it as 'Ooh Pos Pee Cee'.

Before we get to each of these steps, let us first understand, how to deal with what other people want.

Chapter 2

HOW TO DEAL WITH
WHAT OTHER PEOPLE WANT

In the process of managing people you have to often deal with / decipher what others want. Thus, as a manager, your effectiveness and success in dealing with your people depends upon how well you are able to understand their needs and motivate them. This is the basis of minimizing conflict and stress in any group. When dealing with people it is also important to understand and control the impact of informal cliques. In some cases, the authority of the clique may equal or exceed your own. Understanding the extent and source of your managerial authority is an important requirement for being effective.

Let us discuss these topics in order to establish a successful pattern for dealing with people at different levels in an organization.

Understanding Common Human Needs

A group of men were trapped in a mine. After preliminary and cautious excavations, a narrow passage was created through which air could reach them. This passage could not be enlarged as there was the possible danger of the entire mine shaft collapsing. After having been in the mine for over two days, the men were hungry. They started clamoring for food. When it did not become possible to send them food for another two days, their shrieks and screams for food could be heard through the flimsy air passage. A thin pipe was inserted through the air passage pipe and now juice could be delivered to the famished men. Being assured that both air and food were possible, the men then became really concerned about their safety. They sent out pleas to get them out as soon as possible and urged the team to be careful so that in the process of excavation they are not buried alive.

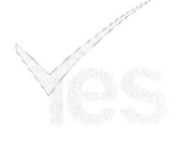

They were reassured through loudspeakers that special equipment was on its way and that they would be rescued shortly. As soon as the rescue operations were on and there was no doubt left that the men would be rescued, they enquired whether there were newspapermen on-site to record their unique survival and the tremendous trauma they had been through. When they came to the surface, they were photographed and interviewed. In a final gesture of demands, they met the General Manager of the mine to suggest that they be employed differently, in better positions ofcourse, in the same organizations.

The above example illustrates what Maslow termed as the hierarchy of human needs. In the Heirarchy of human needs, Maslow considers physiological drives as the most fundamental cause for motivation of human behaviour. As in the example, for the men trapped in the mine, initially, food became the most important concern. The hard fact of the matter is that physiological drives for food and sustenance are essential to the very maintenance of life. In Maslow's model, we see man as a wanting being, striving to satisfy many different needs. These needs have been expressed as a hierarchy, with their order of progression as follows:

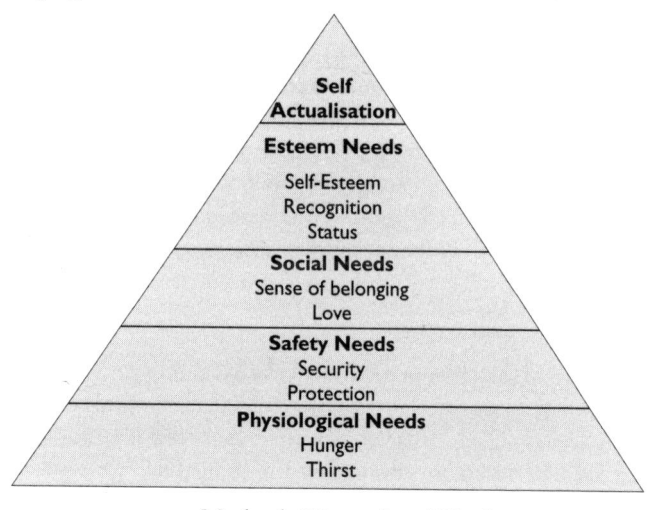

Maslow's Hierarchy of Needs

1. Physiological (Need for the basics – air, water and food)
2. Safety (Need for a safe, familiar and predictable environment)
3. Love (Need for affection and belongingness)
4. Esteem (Need for self-respect and recognition)
5. Self-actualization (Need to do and be what corresponds to an individual's inherent capabilities)

Most of us have or develop all these drives / needs to some extent. However, the order and motivational pull of each need differs with time and situation.

Do all individuals in your contact have the same needs? Clearly, they don't. Even though physiological, safety, love, etc.. need structures (in particular subcultures and cultures) tend to be similar, they still vary with individuals because each individual has a unique personality. In this context, one can look at any individual personality in relation to the particular order and strength of each need. For instance, an artist may place self-actualization, in terms of creativity, high on his hierarchy of needs; that is, this need must be satisfied before he thinks of esteem, status or power.

Some people's needs are more basic. Other observers have related needs such as sex & altruism to the basic five level model of Maslow. Thus, you can look upon sex as a vehicle for need satisfaction, ranging from simple physiological drives to aspirational need for affiliation and power. Similarly, altruism may be an ego drive reflecting the need for affection and achievement.

Furthermore, the order of people's needs may vary under different circumstances. Despite its limitations, the concept of the need hierarchy is useful for the manager. You will discover that, when lower level needs are relatively satisfied, they become less effective as motivators. An individual is motivated mainly by the next / upper level of unsatisfied need. Gratified needs in a sense disappear. A hungry man may work hard for food but once fed, he will no longer work for food. Once a need is fully met with, it is not motivating. However, an individual may have his needs partially met. In such a case, all such needs will motivate this individual in proportion to the unmet level of each need.

As a manager, you can attempt to influence behaviour of your work group by considering what needs are relatively unsatisfied. You may find people in your work group seem to need status, respect, affection or self-actualization. These can then serve as levers for motivating the individuals concerned. Many managers neglect to meet the unfulfilled higher level needs of their employees. The traditional management tendency has been to emphasize financial incentives. This incentive can only partially satisfy the esteem and recognition needs of individuals. Only when the workers badly need money, it works as a motivator.

Therefore, it is often more effective for you, to motivate people through measures such as showing your confidence and trust to the deserving;

providing a system for continuously recognizing good individual and group performance; introducing flexibility in work allocation and assignments to utilize the best abilities of your group members, and so on. These satisfy the need for affiliation, esteem and to some extent, the need for self-actualization. This can be more motivating than the lure of more money, especially, once a person is earning enough to adequately provide for such needs as food and shelter.

Therefore, beyond a certain income level, the motivation to work hard provided through opportunities for group affiliation and recognition (love and esteem needs) tends to be highly effective as compared to the attraction of further monetary gain.

The famous experiments at the Hawthorne Plant of Western Electric, demonstrated that money, as an incentive resulting from production bonuses, quotas and so on, motivates individual employees only up to a certain degree. Scientific experiments observed a steep rise in the productivity of the employees who were consciously being studied in the Hawthorne experiments, regardless of experimental conditions. Why were they suddenly so productive? Such employees felt they were part of a special group of people, and, being aware that their performance was being recognized, they happily produced much more than they had done in the past. When the work studies were analyzed, it motivated the workers to produce to their full capacity, resulting in a sharp rise in productivity.

You can benefit greatly by recognizing the non-financial motivators in order to meet the higher needs of other people.

Understanding Employee Motivation

Let us find out how work is related to meeting the various needs of individuals, and how you can motivate people in an organizational environment.

Undoubtedly, a job is directly related to providing for physiological necessities and satisfying safety and security needs. But what about the next, higher levels on the need hierarchy? Does an ordinary job have any relationship to a person's social needs for affiliation, membership, affection and love? Recent experience has shown that it certainly does.

One of the interesting findings of the Hawthorne Plant studies was that many workers limited their personal effort in order to maintain their membership in an informal social structure. They did not want to outshine their friends, even to earn a production bonus. To them, the desire for communication, support and friendship with associates on the job was more important than that little bit of extra money they could have earned.

A job provides two ways of satisfying the need for affiliation in an individual: First, by providing for the maintenance of a family, and second, by establishing social relations with fellow employees. Thus, social relationships and informal groups can be work motivators if they satisfy the need for affiliation for different employees. If, as a manager, you foster and encourage this, it will aid the commitment and performance of your group.

A job can also provide social esteem, status or prestige. A manager should always co-relate with the title, pay, authority and status symbols amongst his subordinates.

The regional office of a large insurance company was set-up keeping maximum space economy as a priority. Clerks, secretaries, representatives, supervisors, claim men and department heads were all seated at similar desks, row after row. Thomas, the regional manager, was having difficulty with superior morale. Though the more senior and able employees had suitable titles and got more money, they were dissatisfied. Thomas discovered that the principle cause of dissatisfaction was the lack of physical manifestation of status differences, and he decided to introduce the required status differences. He provided individual offices to give quiet privacy to the departmental heads. The supervisors were given additional facilities to make their working conditions efficient and more dignified. This had a tremendous impact - it improved the supervisory morale and superior-subordinate relations.

Employees also derive the satisfaction of self-actualization from their jobs when jobs are designed for individuals, rather than individuals fitted into rigid job descriptions. Perhaps the term self-actualization is too ambiguous in characterizing an important higher need of employees. Therefore, some managers and psychologists have identified three higher needs within self-actualization - need for competence, power and achievement.

Undoubtedly, a major contribution to self-esteem can come from competent performance in one's job. In fact, the drive for self-esteem and competence is instinctive in good workmanship – a human characteristic untapped by most managers. Most men want to feel that they are contributing members of society. There is much satisfaction derived from the dependence and gratitude of others. It give you a sense of being indispensable and therefore a higher self-esteem.

Even so, the drive for competence is mainly internal. You will often notice that as one acquires social esteem his focus shifts from being other-directed and he becomes more inner-directed in an effort to further satisfy himself. He cares less about what others think of his work, more about what he thinks. Thus, successful employees tend to become more individualistic and resist managerial conformity. As long as the manager can keep the competence drive of such employees moving in a positive manner, he will get good performance. Such employees show a high need for achievement.

Both the need for power and the need for achievement are characteristic drives to exceptional performance. The need for achievement is manifested in efforts to meet standards of excellence. The high achiever has a basic attitude towards life - when challenged; he tries harder and demands more of himself. Therefore, he accomplishes more. The achievement oriented person wants tangible rewards, but he does not regard them as essential. He takes a special joy in winning or in competing successfully with a tough standard. In general, individuals with a high level of achievement motivation are more consistent, realistic and action-minded than individuals with other kinds of motivational patterns. Low achievers, on the other hand, will not project any optimism or positive imagination.

As a manager, you can attempt to estimate and evaluate the achievement drive within different people. Those that demonstrate high achievement drives should be given greater responsibilities and the opportunity to meet performance targets. In fact, the need for achievement may be the most important factor in the success of a person.

Motivation At Work

It was the last Douglas Macgregor who first pointed out that managers too often assume that employees view work as punishment. Therefore, they tend to motivate employees through external controls and threats of punishments with regards to the job. He called these his Theory X assumptions. The carrot and stick means of motivation which goes along with Theory X works reasonably well under certain conditions. Willingness to hire, high wages and promises of promotion serve as carrots. Threats to sack, suspensions without pay and so on are sticks. To a certain degree, the means of satisfying an employee's physiological and safety needs can be provided or withheld by the manager. Employment, wages, working conditions and benefits are such means. By these means you, as a manager, can control an individual working for you as long as he is struggling for subsistence.

But the carrot and stick approach does not work at all, once an employee has reached an adequate subsistence level and is motivated primarily by higher needs. You cannot provide your employee with a sense of self-respect or respect from his colleagues, or with the satisfaction of self-fulfillment. You can only create conditions so that the employee is encouraged and enabled to seek such rewards for himself. These conditions can be created when Theory Y assumptions of Macgregor are applied. These assumptions recognize that employees do not inherently dislike work. Work is a natural phenomenon, just as play or rest. Furthermore, incontrast to Theory X, the following additional five assumptions are often made:

1. Control and threat of punishment are not the only means of generating efforts toward organizational objectives. An employee will largely self- direct and self-control himself in the service of objectives to which he is committed.
2. The greater the significance of the rewards, the greater the commitment of employees to objectives. Amongst the more significant rewards are satisfaction of ego and self-actualization needs.
3. The average employee, under proper conditions, will not only accept but seek responsibility.
4. Imagination and creativity for solving organizational problems is widely spread among the employees of an organization. The more the manager applies the concept of participative management the more he can utilize the capabilities of his employees.
5. In the existing work environment, generally, the potential abilities of the average employee are only partially utilized.

Does this mean that under Theory Y, you, as a manager, exercise no control over your people? These assumptions of Theory Y by no means imply that the removal of all control is necessary. They do indicate, however, the possibility of human growth and development, and stress adaptiveness rather than a single absolute form of control. They do point toward the possibility and advantages of the involvement of employees, under favourable conditions and implementation of objectives. As a manager, your understanding and application of Theory Y assumptions will not only equip you to deal with what other people's needs are, but will also enable you to motivate them effectively.

It is important at this stage for you to clearly distinguish between different needs and their motivation in the work environment. Frederick Herzberg, as research director of the Psychological Service of Pittsburgh, conducted an elaborate study of accounting and engineering personnel to determine the factors that satisfy and those that dissatisfy employees. He reported that employees in both groups cited factors inherent in performing work as satisfying and factors surrounding work as dissatisfying. Thus achievement, recognition, and work itself are satisfiers. Working conditions, company policy, administration and interpersonal relations are dissatisfiers. Herzberg reports that an increase in the satisfier is associated with improving performance on the job. For this reason he calls the satisfiers motivators. The dissatisfying elements in the work environment are termed by him as hygiene factors, as implied in preventive medicine. In other words, the removal of dissatisfiers prevents dissatisfaction but does not mean more motivation (just as hygiene may help prevent infection but does not inherently mean more health). The primary implication of Herzberg's work for the manager is that improving interpersonal relations in his group are good only in so far that dissatisfaction is minimized. But to motivate the people in his group, he needs to design jobs and allocate work so as to appeal to their higher level needs.

Overemphasis on improving the hygiene factors for a group of employees will not give the desired motivational effect that a manager may be anticipating. To really motivate employees one can develop opportunities through their jobs to give them a sense of achievement, recognition and other higher level needs. Improvements in the hygiene factors are most beneficial when the motivators or job expectation factors are satisfactory.

Although, the motivators or job expectation factors differ with different employees, generally every employee falls into one of the following three categories:

1. An employee with a truncated need structure: Such an employee is influenced only by the lower level needs and therefore, can only be motivated with money or minimum social satisfaction through his job that is, friendships with co-workers. It is irrelevant whether the job or the manager offers opportunities for competence, power or achievement. In fact, these opportunities may confuse and upset such an employee, particularly if the manager attempts to focus on the satisfaction of any of the higher-level needs. As a manager, your effectiveness with such an employee will depend upon how well you

exercise your authority over the means to satisfy the lower needs, such as pay, working conditions, working hours and so on.

2. An employee with developed higher needs which he pursues away from his job: Such a person has been taught or believes that a job is an unpleasant necessity, and work, a punishment. He will therefore be motivated to obtain only money and minimum social satisfaction on the job, and to use the money to satisfy his higher needs (through a hobby, spiritual groups, athletics and so on). It is irrelevant whether the job or the manager offers opportunities for competence, power or achievement. As a manager, your effectiveness will depend upon how well you exercise your authority over the means to satisfy his lower needs.

3. An employee with developed higher needs which he pursues on the job: Such an individual believes that a job can provide opportunities for competence, power and achievement. If the job or the manager does not offer these opportunities, the employee will probably retaliate with behaviour detrimental to himself as well as to the organization. On the other hand, if you, as a manager, provide him with opportunities for the fulfillment of these higher needs, he will be immensely motivated, and will generate behaviour that is constructive to both himself and the organization.

On the basis of the above categorization, you as a manager, can estimate the needs of each of your employees. This will enable you to deal with their wants more effectively and thereby motivate them towards better performance on the job.

Minimizing Conflict And Stress In Your Group
In addition to the need for motivating employees, a manager is often faced with a situation of dysfunctional stress and conflict in his work group.

What causes stress and conflict in a work group? There are generally two major reasons. The first is interpersonal conflict. Managers often blame this on personality problems or the incompetence of individuals. It is not uncommon to find two employees who have difficulty in cooperating with each other. While it is true that some people cause stress and conflict by their nature and mannerisms, the more common reason for interpersonal conflict is frustration. This arises when an internal barrier stands between a motivated employee and his goals. When the barrier is not overcome, or when the motivation to do something which the barrier is obstructing becomes stronger, then a number of responses may result. In the work situation, the barrier may be attacked symbolically (e.g., throwing darts at a picture of the boss) or organizationally (by work slowdown, forgetting or sabotage). Although frustration is the major cause for aggression, it may also occur from an employee's power motives and a certain love for conflict.

Although, as mentioned above, people are sometimes the source of conflict and stress in the group. The second and more prevalent cause of conflict arises from faulty communication flow in the organization. Unfortunately, this is often overlooked by the practising manager, resulting in continued stress and conflict in his work group. Organization structure is the formal design of work flow, and largely determines the flow of interactions in the organization. It spells out who initiates and who responds, who sees whom, how often and so on. When these structurally determined communication patterns conflict with employees personality patterns, stress is produced. This stress can be minimized only through a change in behaviour.

> *Inder an experienced manager, was transferred to a new department, but continued to spend accustomed amount of time with his subordinates. His new position, however, required that Inder frequently meet and consult with his fellow department heads. When he neglected to do this because of his habitual preoccupation with his department work, other departmental heads started pressurizing him. As the new pressures built up, Inder was quick to realize that he must modify his interaction pattern to reduce tension and dissatisfaction, or his organization position would be threatened. He therefore, began to devote more time to working with his fellow departmental heads.*

There are three interaction patterns in an organization that cause detrimental stress:
  1.   Uni-flow interaction
  2.   Insufficient and irregular interaction
  3.   Changing and unpredictable interaction

1. Uni-flow Interaction
Any working relationship in which the interaction flow between individuals is fragmented and infrequent tends to generate stress and conflict. This is illustrated by the following example.

> *The Sales department of a large engineering factory making castings, tools and sewing machine components was divided into four sections – export, in-country distribution, claims & replacement and shipping. It was a sales-service department, as the actual selling function was handled by the field sales organization. The work flow in the department was such that there was only*

intermittent interaction between the supervisor, Sunil, of the claims and replacement section, and Rajiv, supervisor of the shipping section. These supervisors could not get along with each other, and each one was quick to blame the other whenever a claim for replacement had to be processed. Ratan, the sales manager, thought this trouble was a problem of the two strong and conflicting personalities involved, since Sunil and Rajiv got along very well with the rest of the department staff. Ratan decided to redistribute the work load in his department by promoting the supervisors of the in-country distribution section out into the field sales organization. He then made Sunil supervisor of a combined in-country distribution, claims and replacement section. Sunil was a well qualified supervisor. The only thing which worried Ratan was whether Sunil would be able to improve his working relationship with the supervisor of the shipping section, Rajiv. However, the changed work flow in the department brought these two supervisors into regular contact everyday. This resulted in the two of them developing a mutual trust and reliability within a few weeks, and practically removed their stressful conflicts.

2. Insufficient and irregular interaction

Inadequate interaction does not give an opportunity for individuals to develop mutual trust and understanding. This is one of the reasons why the staff and line groups generate conflict and stress in each other. The interaction between them tends to be intermittent, which does not help to remove mutual doubts of each other's authority and capability. You can help to minimize stress and conflict under conditions of inadequate interaction. This is how you do it:-

i)   Redesign the work allocations to give opportunities for greater work oriented interaction between employees.
ii) Encourage social interaction through group activities outside the work environment, without letting it become too demanding.

There is widespread agreement that an adequate amount of social interaction is essential to keep stress and conflict at a minimum within a working group. Thus you have to be aware that inadequacy both in work communication and social interactions can be stressful in a work group.

3. Changing interaction

Employees do not like adjusting to unexpected changes in initiation and response patterns. In any work situation, over a period of time, people become familiar with one another's working habits, approach to problems, type of suggestions each would automatically accept or reject and so on. Frequent transfers of personnel should therefore be avoided, as they upset these relationships and require energy to be put in building up new relationships between the new set of employees.

Changes in procedures, policy, technology and so on, also modify interaction patterns. When these changes are introduced unilaterally without consultation and apparent justification, they tend to generate stress and conflict in the work environment. An example of how dramatically a simple procedure can affect interaction pattern is illustrated below.

Sanjay Kumar, manager of a development department, was concerned about the low productivity of his department. His engineers often complained about the time they had to spend assisting sales people to solve quotation problems. The salesmen individually consulted the development engineers whenever they felt it was necessary. Sanjay issued a departmental order that all salesmen would have to record their times in and out of the development department, by making an entry in a register. Obviously, the purpose of the register was to measure the amount of time the salesmen spent in the development department.

The very first sales executive who entered the development department after the order was issued was advised to sign the register. The sales executive ignored this advice and went on ahead to the engineer he wanted to see. However, the engineer refused to discuss anything unless the sales executive signed the register. An argument started, ending up in the sales executive stomping away with indignation. The development manager then went to see the marketing manager, and demanded that all sales personnel sign the register. This resulted in all the sales personnel agreeing to sign the register when ordered by their superior. Actually, however, many of them ceased consulting the development department. Communication flow between the two departments was drastically reduced. The company objectives obviously suffered because the sales personnel stopped quoting on products requiring engineering assistance in order to avoid the development department as much as possible. The sales personnel were not so against having their visits recorded as they were against the manner in which change was introduced. They felt that the development department assistant or secretary could record visits in the register. It was not so important. Furthermore, if they or their manager had been consulted prior to the change, then things would have been different and they would have cooperated.

The above incident shows how a simple but sudden change in communication pattern, when improperly introduced, can generate extreme stress and conflict. A manager, therefore, has to be perceptive enough to understand that a necessary change in interacting patterns, whenever necessary, is introduced after consultation and discussion with those who are going to be affected by the change.

As a manager, you can take the following approaches to minimize conflict and stress in your group:

    i)   **Work allocation:** When necessary, adjust work allocation to reorient conflicting personalities. Motivate desirable organization behaviour, such as cooperation at the time of reorientation.

ii) **Interaction and Communication:** Check that communication flow in the group is not uni-directional, insufficient or subject to sudden change. If so, then reorient communication patterns and work allocation so that communication becomes two way or multi-directional, regular, adequate and predictable. Also encourage social interaction to supplement work related interaction.

iii) **Group Cohesiveness:** Increase group cohesiveness through such measures as free and informal communications, stable membership, common values and standards, mutual dependency and individual participation in the group's objective setting and implementation.

iv) **Coordination & Mediation:** Competition and conflict will tend to appear in any working group because of the political nature of man. You have to take the responsibility to coordinate and mediate amongst the conflicting interests which may be present in your group. In doing so you may be able to fruitfully employ one of the three approaches mentioned above.

Generally, managers tend to treat conflict and stress in the group as having to do primarily with personality problems. They neglect to consider other causes such as faulty work allocations and lack of coordination within different pressure groups. As a manager, you can minimize stress and conflict in your group by following the four approaches mentioned above.

Controlling The Impact Of Informal Cliques

We must remember that in dealing with what other people want, as a manager it will be to your advantage to know about and understand the informal groups within your organization. Only by doing so, will you be in a position to control the situation.

Man is basically a social animal. Therefore, informal interaction as an extension of the organization is a common human practice. It is a primary fact that men live in groups in the company of other people. It has been somewhat traditional, however, to view informal cliques or groups in the organization as being essentially detrimental. Recent study has revealed the glaring contrast that exists between the behaviour of prisoners of war during the Second World War and the Korean War in 1950.

Jubilation and happiness characterized the American prisoners freed from Nazi Germany, whereas sullenness and enmity were typical of those freed from Korea.

Investigations indicated differences in the organization and treatment of prisoners in Nazi Germany and communist Korea. In the Nazi camps, the prisoners were dealt with through a military structure. The imprisoned officers were required to police and maintain the internal organization. After interrogation, the prisoners were returned to the same group - the expectation being that the unfortunate, tortured men would serve as examples to frighten others into talking. Despite the mistreatment, bad food and clothing, there was a relatively low death rate, many escaped and there were hardly any instances of revolt.

The conditions in Korea were different. The prisoners were fed and clothed like the guards. In prison camps, officers were separated from enlisted men, and sometimes lower ranking men were intentionally placed in charge of noncommissioned officers to disrupt both formal and informal acceptance of leadership. Prisoners were periodically transferred, and groups systematically broken up to avoid the development of a military or informal organization amongst the prisoners. Except in a few extreme cases, the Koreans generally used relatively little physical torture. After a prisoner was interrogated, he was made to appear elsewhere in the camp, seemingly well, and usually with new clothes. This meant that the prisoners did not know what to expect, and they could not brace themselves psychologically. Furthermore, this created distrust and suspicion in the behaviour between friends. All this created a low morale, high death rate, few escapes, general ill health and instances of compromising acceptance.

What does an informal clique or group really offer to an employee? It offers three things as brought out in the above example.

1. **The fulfillment of social needs**: Practical experience between work groups indicates that employees, who have no opportunity for social contact, find their work unsatisfying. This may reflect itself in low production, absenteeism and high employee turnover. Elton Mayo, observed that the employees of a textile plant who worked in isolated jobs were dissatisfied and failed to meet production standards. When the textile company permitted such employees to take rest periods as a group, both satisfaction and production increased. This holds true at all times and in different places. Hospitals have discovered that maids feel uncomfortable when they work only in the company of doctors and nurses. However, when three or four of them are grouped together as a team, a more efficient job is done. It has been found that the enjoyment and assistance derived from informal associations on the job help to make it more pleasant, and thereby more productive.

2. **Identification and emotional support:** Self-image is derived from social image. In an office or on a shop floor, the informal group can guide the individual vis-a-vis desirable and undesirable behaviour. Even where established rules exist, a question always remains about the extent to which everyone is expected to live by the letter of the law. How much time should one take for a coffee break? What papers need to be marked to the general manager? Do all copies need to be shown to the boss? What is the best time to get sanctions on important work orders? The informal and formal groups both provide guidelines to employees in terms of not only written policies but also in terms of what is actually acceptable.

    The emotional support, which both formal and informal group identification provides, encourages people to excel, in order to bring a good name to the organisation. The manager, therefore, need not be afraid of informal cliques. If approached positively, informal cliques can serve to facilitate desirable and acceptable organizational performance. They can provide emotional support imperative for consistent productivity.

3. Assistance in meeting goals: Groups, both formal and particularly informal, tend to assist their individual members in solving specific problems. It has been found that employees tend to turn to their fellow employees / friends for help first, as opposed to going to their manager. The point I am trying to make is that when the informal groups in your organization have goals in harmony with the needs of the organization, then they aid in the achievement of managerial objectives.

Informal groups are composed of employees who (i) frequently communicate with each other on the job and (ii) have similar likes and dislikes. As a manager, you will have to deal with informal cliques simply because they always emerge from the formal organization.

Therefore, learn to accept your people not only as individuals but also as components of impact groups. It is particularly important to understand the relationship between formal and informal status systems and to try and maintain continuity between them. Thus, an employee who is unofficially recognized as being the leader of the informal group should be groomed into formal leadership. It would be inviting trouble to disregard such informal leadership between employees and appoint people on other considerations from within the group into lead or supervisory positions. An employee who is not accepted as being deserving of a lead role in the informal group, will not get the respect or cooperation necessary for him to be effective organizationally.

Therefore, recognize and accept the assistance of informal groups. Going a step further, it would even be to your advantage to encourage the formation of informal cliques where the nature of individual jobs is such that it would not foster such formation.
Ways by which a manager can influence these groups positively is :
1. Through his leadership.
2. Changing or redesigning work-flow patterns and organizational structure.
3. Using the principles of managing change
4. By sensitivity training to improve relationships.
I re-emphasise that a manager will benefit by recognizing and accepting informal groups as an essential part of any organization. By controlling their impact as discussed, he can do good to both employee and organizational needs.

The Source Of Your Managerial Authority
In dealing with the needs of your employees and those of the formal and informal groups which exist in the organization, it is beneficial to keep in mind the source of your managerial authority.

The obvious source is your official position in the organization given to you by the top management. This position gives you the power of rewarding and punishing employees thus inducing them to obey you. Other sources of your authority are your own personal charisma, leadership traits and the socio-cultural difference arising from your experience and social status. But perhaps the least understandable and one of the most important sources of your authority is the acceptance awarded to you by your subordinates. As long as your communications are objectively based on better and more complete information (as is usually the case), there will be a cooperative personal attitude amongst the individuals working with you. Thus, for your authority to be truly effective, you need to be the center of the system and there needs to be an attitude of personal cooperation between your employees. Both factors are interdependent on each other.

To strengthen your position of authority in a practical way, you would need to make sure that you get adequate information from the organization structure, so that orders or instructions automatically receive a high response of cooperation and acceptance by your employees. When making a decision or passing instructions it helps check your basis; to review if there is any information you are not getting. If so, then arrange to get this information to further increase your credibility and authority. This will invariably enable you to offset a precedence with your people more effectively. Moreover, with respect to authority, employees can be categorized into three kinds:

Employee 1: The Dependent
He feels comfortable having others as leaders and in following all rules and regulations.

Employee 2: The Counter Dependent
He develops feelings of discomfort towards people in authority and towards following rules and regulations.

Employee 3: The Independent
He has no preconceived feelings for or against people in authority and with regards to rules and regulations. He measures each situation and manager without stereotyping, that is, objectively.

Employees 1 and 2 tend to alternate between the extremes of submission and rebellion. Imagine an employee says that he views all superiors as being helpful. Since in reality, this is not the case, he will cling to this view on the surface, but will have an underlying distrust of all superiors. Therefore, he will tend to move within the extremes of submission and rebellion. The same is true of the employee who believes that all authority systems are bad. Since in reality, there are some good leaders, he would also let his attitude vary between rebellion and submissiveness. Employees who fall in the third category are the most productive. Their attitude is not preconceived and therefore does not vary in the unrealistic and undesirable range that swings from complete submissiveness to chaotic rebellion. They are realistic at most situations, particularly where there is need for greater understanding and cooperation.

As a leader, you need to help the dependents and the counter dependents discover the need to change their preconceived notions. This can be achieved by discussing matters individually and proposing the right approach. A more effective method is the use of sensitivity training which is discussed in Chapter 11.

Your ability to strengthen your sources of authority, as well as to categorize and improve the attitude of your people towards authority and its system will brew greater credibility and encourage better results.

Dealing With Employees

How can you be democratic in your dealing with subordinates while maintaining the necessary authority and control in the organization? This is a problem faced by all modern managers.

The answer cannot be a rigid one, as it needs to be relevant to various situations and needs. A good pattern of behaviour to follow while dealing with subordinates is to use different leadership styles to suit different situations. To be more specific, let us see what are these different leadership patterns :

On one extreme is the possibility of the manager himself identifying a problem, considering alternatives and choosing one of them for implementation. On the other extreme is the manager who sets general guidelines consistent with the organization procedure, and then turns the decisions over to the group, of which he may consider himself as a member. On encounters such a pattern only occasionally. It is particularly effective for research development groups where a team identifies and diagnoses the problem, develops alternative solutions and then decides on what appears to be the best course of action.

In a practical situation, how should a manager decide on the type of leadership pattern he should use? Leadership style depends upon three major considerations:

1. **The leader's value system and personality:** A leader's own convictions and opinions pertaining to the level of involvement his subordinates should have in decision-making influences the end spectrum. Other considerations are his confidence in his subordinates and how secure he feels when dealing with uncertainty.

2. **The nature and behaviour of subordinates:** A leader can permit greater freedom to his subordinates if certain conditions exist. These conditions are discussed in detail in Chapter 10, but essentially center around the following prerequisite, viz., that the subordinates must be ready and willing to assume responsibility for decision-making. If, on the other hand, they have no desire for and have learned to expect authoritative directives, it would only upset them if they are requested to participate in the decision-making process.

3. **The nature of the situation:** The considerations here are the type of organization and its existing value systems, the ability of the

employees to work effectively as a group and the nature of the problem. Employees may not have the necessary experience or information to take certain types of decisions. The key question for the manager to always ask is whether he has heard everyone who has the necessary knowledge and experience to make a significant contribution. Recent experience in managerial effectiveness has shown that a fairly high degree of subordinate centered behaviour leads to higher employee motivation, readiness of subordinates to accept change, improvement in the quality of managerial decision, development of teamwork and also the individual development of employees.

At the same time, while establishing a successful leadership pattern to exclusively perceive the three major considerations outlined above, is not enough. the key is to behave appropriately, in the light of the total situation. Thus, if direction is in order, the leader is able to direct, but where considerable participative freedom is necessary, he is able to provide such participative leadership. It is important that the leader conveys to his subordinates whatever leadership pattern he may be using. As an example, if he decides to take a certain decision, but his subordinate group gets the impression that he has delegated this authority, confusion and resentment are likely to follow. It is therefore highly important for a leader to be honest and clear in describing what authority and what role is he asking his subordinates to carry out while solving a particular problem. Clarity leads to efficient and quick disposal of work.

Dealing With Superiors

It is, of course, obvious that your success partly depends upon the ability to deal effectively with one's superiors. Sometimes this is not easy, particularly when your boss has a strong personality or conflicting likes and dislikes and number of (what you might consider) grave weaknesses; such as a bad temper, inconsistency in approaching similar situations, and so on.

How do you deal with such a boss? Your pattern of dealing with a bad boss as well as a good boss can be based around a cardinal principle in dealing with people.

Emphasize and benefit from people's strengths. List in our own mind what some of the strengths of your boss are. Then put an accent on these strengths while dealing with him. If he has an excellent technical knowledge, then benefit from that by emphasizing the solution to technical problems as an important area in your dealings with him. Spare him from suffering in the areas where he is weak by keeping those dealings to a minimum.

This will have two major advantages:
  i) You will benefit by getting good decisions in the strong areas of your boss.
  ii) Your boss will feel more comfortable and think better of you as he will be able to communicate with you easily and without stress. This is because it is simple human nature for people to like those who support and share their strengths.

Everyone has strengths and weaknesses. It is a good idea to accentuate the strengths of your superiors and overlook their weaknesses, as far as possible. Also the pleasure in discussing the weaknesses of one's superiors with other employees is not without danger. Constructive criticisms and discussions on the request of the boss is the best opportunity to go over his strengths and weaknesses in a positive manner.

It is also in the interest of every manager to help his superiors move up in areas where they offer no direct competition to him. An upward movement in the organization does generally result in opening various opportunities and faster promotions which may not have been foreseen initially.

Your pattern of dealing with your superiors should practically reflect your appreciation of their strong areas, your ability to take care of other areas without bringing attention to your superiors' weaknesses in these areas and your support of their movement upwards in the organization structure. With this approach, your superiors will help you get the results you want.

Now lets see how to get the best results from people.

Chapter 3

HOW TO GET THE BEST RESULTS FROM YOUR PEOPLE

When it comes to managing people, executives have found the following points to be helpful. These are four approaches that can enable you to get the best results from your people.

1. It pays to gear efforts to results rather than to work. This means focusing on the contributions which each of their team members (superiors, colleagues and subordinates) make and can make to achieve desired goals. It starts with establishing individual contributions rather than the work to be done or its techniques and tools.
2. Best results are obtained by building on strong points – their own strong points, the strengths of their superiors, colleagues, subordinates and the situation itself. Do not let weaknesses or impossibility of tasks distract your efforts.
3. To get superior performance and outstanding results, concentrate on a few major areas. Set up priorities and follow through on the decisions. Understand how to make meetings effective as well as productive by using the principle of contribution. Clarify the purpose of meetings before holding them, and go through to achievement.
4. To execute effective decisions, know how to balance democratic behaviour with getting tough when necessary. Tailor-make team leadership to suit different situations.

Let us now see how these approaches can be put to use in any organizational setting.

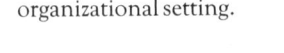

Focusing on the Contribution of Each Member

The focus on contribution is the key to getting the best results from your people. You have to ask yourself how best you can contribute in your present position to the organization. How can your subordinates, colleagues and superiors contribute individually in their relationship with you and you with them? What contributions can accrue from meetings, reports and the management tools and techniques you apply? The organizational mechanics, chain of command, office procedures and all efforts in themselves are of no advantage. It is the results from the efforts which matter. Hence with every individual in your team, with every situation, with every meeting and in general, with every organizational activity, it is necessary to think about contributions rather than efforts.

Despite the obviousness in the logic that results should be emphasized over efforts, most executives get wrapped up in matters of authority and in their own efforts. This is illustrated in the following case example.

A well known management consultant rates executives quite accurately from the answers he receives to the following question: "What do you do to justify your being on the payroll?" The great majority answer in the following manner: "I am in charge of the sales force," or "I have 900 people working under me." or "I run the administration department of the company." Such answers stress downward authority and focus on efforts. They do not reflect results or contributions. Those executives who are on their way up and have a history of success, look upon their jobs differently. They are likely to say the following: "I am responsible for meeting the targeted sales of the company's products and generating customer satisfaction," or "I am responsible for the efficient production of the company's products," or "It's my job to give our managers the information required to make the right decisions!" During the course of his interviews, when he finds executives focusing on contribution and responsibility for results, he recommends them as "top management" material. Accordingly, the persons who focus on efforts and stress their downward authority are "subordinate" material, no matter how high their title and rank, they do not hold themselves accountable for the performance of the whole.

The focus on contribution turns the executive's attention away from his own department towards the performance of the whole. Such an executive is likely to think about what relationships his skills, function, specialty and department have to better the overall organization and its purpose. As a result, what he does and gets others to do will not be out of phase with the main objectives of the organization.

In dealing with your immediate group of subordinates, as well as with various other individuals in the organization, good working relationships are important. Focus on contribution in your own work. This will make relationships productive - the only way to good working relationships. Pleasant words and warm feelings are meaningless, if there is no achievement in a work focused and task focused relationship. On the contrary, an occasional rough word will not damage a relationship that is based on results and accomplishments. In a study of successful managers who inspired deep devotion and true affection in all who worked for them, Peter Drucker points out a common trait - all of them built their relationships with their emphasis on productive working. In fact, this common emphasis by otherwise widely differing managerial personalities made them well known in industry for their wonderful ability to manage people and keep organization morale high.

To establish contributions from subordinates, it is best to take a direct approach. You can ask your people for answers to the following questions:
What are the results for which you feel you should be held accountable?
What should be expected of you?
Can we utilize your knowledge and ability better?

These questions can be put to all the employees in the form of a questionnaire and the answers can be discussed with each employee in individual sessions. You, of course, will have the right and the responsibility to judge the validity of the proposed contribution. You may be amazed to find that the objectives set forth by some employees will project opportunities and results, far in excess to expectations. Such increased targets, whenever feasible, should be supported. You will also benefit in this exercise, as you will become aware of how your employees perceive needs and opportunities. This common sharing of mutual concerns will make you and your group more cohesive and make your job of establishing individual contribution goals more effective and realistic.

Ask the same questions of yourself. This will foster individual self-development both personally and in the eyes of others. By focusing on contribution, employees will analyze the self-development they need, they will think about what additional knowledge and skills need to be acquired and what personal goals should be set. You will find that other subordinates, colleagues or superiors will soon follow suit and be stimulated to develop themselves. It has been found that people grow according to the demands they make on themselves. Focusing on contribution serves to do this in a practical manner for both yourself and everyone you work with.

When you inform your superiors and colleagues about the contributions you have promised to make, it will, if necessary, que them to gear themselves up too. Teamwork in your own work group will also increase, as people will now be concerned with how the output of others can be used to make the group's results more effective.

Thus, focusing on the contribution of each member in your work group, including yourself, is a tool to get the best results from your people.

Building on Everyone's Strengths

To get optimum results from people one must use everyone's strong points well, i.e. the strengths of subordinates, associates, superiors and ones own. To make these strengths productive is the key to individual and organization success. Every individual is abundantly endowed with weaknesses. The leader's efforts can make these largely irrelevant by using the strength of each employee as a basis for joint performance. The most practical way of using employee strength is in the process of staffing.

Staffing for results:

Staffing decisions are crucial decisions. All results are obtained through the most important organization resource – high caliber people. The better this resource is allocated to contribution areas or opportunities, the greater the achievement of desired results. For the maximization of results from this resource, it is necessary to practise the following principle:

The top caliber employees must always be allocated to major opportunities or tasks.

One must try to exploit major opportunities with top caliber people. If this resource does not exist, the organization must get it or develop it from within existing human resources. If none appear to be available, the need of the hour is to seek or develop new ones.

All this is easier said than done. It is not easy to staff for performance because of human likes and dislikes, personal considerations, the temptation to diffuse top rate resources rather than to concentrate on them and so on.

Staffing for performance, therefore, makes you impose on yourself the discipline of an objective staffing method called the forced-choice method. To use this approach, you need to take the following steps:

Step 1.   Draw up a list of major opportunities (tasks) and assign a ranking to each, in terms of contributions to desired results. Each opportunity must be ranked without ambiguity.

Step 2. Rank your people / resources by their ability to perform. All top caliber, mediocre and marginal employees must be ranked consecutively.

Step 3. To the highest ranking opportunity or task, allocate all the high ranking human resources that it requires. The next ranking opportunity comes next, and so on. Low ranking opportunities are not to be staffed at the expense of a higher ranking one.

The ranking of people and opportunities or tasks becomes the basic decision in this method of staffing for results.

Once the people and opportunities are matched, efforts can be taken to structure the work organization so as to make strengths productive and weaknesses irrelevant. Let us see how some managers have implemented this approach.

Arun Roy, an Accounts Manager, hired a good tax accountant who was known to have suffered in his private practise due to his inability to get along with people. Arun saw to it that the tax expert got an office area of his own, and initially designed the work flow, so as to shield him from direct contact with other people. The organization saved a record amount in taxes the following year, because the strength of a key employee was concentrated on a desired result opportunity, and his weakness was made largely irrelevant by the "staffing for results" approach of an effective accounts manager.

Building on the strengths of individuals and work teams has thus been a success pattern followed by effective managers in generating optimum performance through their people.

The Importance of Concentration

There are so many different areas of importance that the day by day method of management is no longer adequate. It has become necessary for every manager to reduce the almost limitless number of possible tasks to a manageable number. Because of so many demands, there is need to concentrate important resources on the greatest opportunities and results. In other words, it has become necessary to do the few important things right and with excellence. This can be achieved only through concentration of both people resources and time to produce optimum results.

We have already seen that you can benefit from concentrating your top human resources; similarly, you can get best results by concentrating on doing one important thing at a time. That is the only way that majority of people can achieve excellence in the accomplishment of major opportunities. Concentration of effort is necessary precisely because there are so many tasks clamoring to be done. Doing one thing at a time, results in doing it fast. The more you can concentrate on time, effort and resources, the greater the number and diversity of tasks you can actually accomplish.

Pradeep, a management consultant retained to advice on organization structure revision, was particularly impressed with the way Raj, the general manager of the organization, managed his time. The sessions Pradeep had with Raj were neither too short nor too long, being about 1 ½ hours each. This was a big enough chunk of time to cover everything important, and short enough to avoid repetitive discussions. During these sessions, there was never a phone call or any other personal interruption. Pradeep also discovered that the general manager had a very effective way of consolidating and concentrating chunks of time for major issues and productive tasks. All meetings, reviews, problem sessions and so on were scheduled for two days a week, on Mondays and Thursdays. The mornings of all other days were set aside for consistent work on major issues and productive tasks. The afternoons were left unscheduled for whatever might come up. Of course, many things did come up, such as urgent personnel problems, visits by important customers, trips, emergency production meetings, etc. It was in the mornings of three days a week that Raj concentrated his time only on major result producing issues which made him a highly effective manager.

The manner in which managers concentrate their discretionary time on productive issues is not important – it is what they do that matters. Effective managers control their time management continuously. The process of time management and concentration involves the following four steps:

1. **Know where your time goes:** Before you can attempt to manage and give your time to productive issues, you must know where it goes. The best way to do this is to record how your time is spent. You can do this by keeping a time log yourself, or asking your secretary or assistant to maintain it for you. A two week analysis of your time log will show you how little of your time is being spent on productive matters, and how great a time is being taken up on unimportant and unproductive tasks.

2. **Prune time wasters:** Dispense with tasks which have no bearing on results, where nothing of significance would happen if you didn't do them. These may be speeches, committee memberships, meetings, etc., that contribute little or nothing to your own organizational activity which may be dispensed with. If there are any in your

existing time schedule, don't hesitate to say "no" to them. If you value your time, others will also follow suit.

3. **Delegate tasks:** Estimate what tasks could be done by someone else just as well, if not better. Transfer such tasks from your own work schedule to those who should really be doing them.

4. **Consolidate and give time to productive tasks:** Set aside time in appreciable amounts to be concentrated on major issues in order to produce optimum results. Small increments of time on minor issues will lead to inefficiency and mediocrity, if not worse. Time must be spent in large, continuous and uninterrupted units to accomplish productive and significant tasks.

Thus, the process of concentration both in the area of people resources and time provides for optimum results.

Setting Priorities

It is important to do one thing at a time, but one must know which things to do first and in what priority.

Generally speaking, work pressure determines tasks that need to be done immediately, whereas, other high priority tasks get sacrificed. Pressures always concentrate on yesterdays or the past. Results exist in the future – past achievements and problems should not preoccupy the effective manager.

The best way to set priorities is to do it the hard way, that is.,by first deciding what tasks not to tackle. This is not easy. It is much easier to draw up a nice list of top priorities and then hedge by trying to do a little of everything. This is likely to make everyone happy. Nevertheless, nothing gets done. In order to concentrate on efforts, human resources and time on result producing tasks, the lower ranking or irrelevant tasks must first be eliminated. A task which appears to have no significant impact on the future should be eliminated without fear, as only one of the three things can happen:

1. Nothing
2. It is attended to happen in time automatically during the course of another result producing task.
3. It becomes an important issue in the future, and is attended to be completed then.

Of course, it is necessary to be objective in eliminating tasks – focus on its future impact. Unpleasantness or lack of interest in doing the task, should not be the decision criterion.

Having eliminated tasks which need not be done, you should rank those which need to be undertaken.

These should be done using the following as yardsticks of merit:
- ☞ Rank highest those tasks that produce most results per unit of effort.
- ☞ Pick future-oriented tasks against past-oriented ones.
- ☞ Select tasks that aim high and will make a difference, rather than those that are safe and easy to do.

Remember, it is more productive to convert an opportunity into results than to solve a problem which restores the balance of the past. Problems which need to be solved should certainly be tackled, but they should not be given priority over tasks which will produce results in the future. When the priority graph reverses, the role of a manager becomes mainly that of a problem solver and someone who maintains the working status quo. Such activity does not result in excellent performance. The manager remains behind and is left dealing with the past and the present. The future slips by him, unnoticed.

Research studies in managerial competence have shown that excellence in achievement depends less on technical ability or managerial know how than on the courage to go after opportunities in tasks. This is the only way to get out of mediocrity and achieve managerial excellence.

> The manager of sales coordination for a sewing machine factory, Afsar Khan, was well respected for his ability to handle problems. He had become well-versed in dealing with product allocation, supply demand mismatch, product scheduling, export shipping, customer claims and inland freight problems. It was hard work to tackle the multitude of problems which crept up daily and still keep the products moving to desired locations. There seemed to be no end to the work which needed to be done everyday. So it was with glee that he transferred this work to Suresh, a young manager in the production plant, who accepted an equivalent staff position. The new manager of sales coordination saw tremendous opportunities for results in his new assignment. Suresh realized that problem solving was important, but relegated it in comparison to the opportunities. Because of this, Suresh delegated problem solving activity to his section heads, who consulted him only for problems they couldn't handle themselves. This resulted in excellent performance of the sales coordination department. The young manager generated freight and cost reduction savings to unexpected proportions. Additional revenues from increased exports and freight claims improved the operations of the organization, and his salary was more than doubled. He had risen from mediocrity to excellence, and was earmarked as top management material. This was in large measure because he had the courage to go after opportunities, rather than let himself be bogged down with problem solving.

To achieve excellence in your own work environment, you must decide what really matters and comes first in terms of opportunities. You must become the master of time and events, rather than be dictated by problem solving and other work pressures.

Priorities must be reconsidered and revised in the light of realities. As soon as you accomplish your priority tasks, the priorities of the other tasks before you change and should be revised.

Thus, prioritizing the opportunities before your work group should be a continuous activity. This is necessary if you want outstanding results from your self and your people.

Making Meetings Effective

A large portion of one's time is spent in meetings, reports or presentations – whether with individuals or with groups. For getting best results from others, it is necessary to make such meetings effective.

There are various common sense rules for making group meetings effective:

1. **Plan ahead for the meeting.** Ask for agenda items and /or distribute agenda well in time for others to come adequately prepared for the meeting. Ask people to take specific actions beforehand, such as preparing statistics, interviewing several employees to get reactions on a proposal, etc., whenever necessary.
2. **Guide the meeting on constructive channels.** Avoid it from becoming a battlefield for rivals. Also, do not permit time wasting digressions.
3. **Keep the atmosphere for discussion open.** Encourage people who generally remain quiet to have their say. Relieve tension with a joke or a pleasant story.
4. **Have someone note down the important points.** The attempt should be to record all important suggestions, agreements and actions plans. Descriptions of how the discussions went are not necessary for work meetings.
5. **Take some time to summarize and outline what needs to be done next.** Before the scheduled finish to the meeting, make sure that you summarize the main points and outline what needs to be done next.
6. **Assure follow-up.** Make sure that either you or an assistant, email a list of tasks to be done as a result to the meeting, with names of corresponding individuals responsible for implementation or follow-up. Give dates, wherever desirable and practical, by when these tasks should be completed.

Managers can add to these working guidelines based on their own styles and situations. Nevertheless, the most indispensable point in making meetings effective is to clearly define to your self and to others, its purpose and specific contribution.

Effective managers have a habit of insisting that the purpose be thought of and spelled out before a meeting is called, a report asked for or a presentation organized. Then they insist that the meeting serve the contribution to which it has been committed.

Focusing on contribution encourages relevance of events and teamwork. It helps to overcome the temptation to remain preoccupied with efforts, work relationships, problems & weaknesses, and gets the work group to concentrate on their fundamental commitment to generating results.

Thus, the basic ingredient which you need to use in dealing with meetings, reports and presentations is emphasis on contribution. Determine the contribution desired, and focus on it to make all meetings get you the results you want from your people.

Getting Tough When Necessary

In getting optimum results from people, a manager needs to have a feel for when to use democratic or participative leadership, and when to be tough and assertive. The most desirable approach, of course, depends upon the situation. In general, as a manager you should be both autocratic and democratic in different situations.

In dealing with people, you will generally be faced with one of the following five situations. In each situation, the desirable behaviour which you may plan to project has been spelled out:

1. **Information collection:** These situations cover interviewing new employees, getting staff member reports, hearing union grievances and so on. The recommended behaviour here is participative. You have to get the facts out from others and get them to air their thoughts. Encourage others to speak and be flexible in your reactions to what you hear. Do not impose your thoughts or actions onto others in these situations.

2. **Giving information:** This includes situations such as addressing an employee group, explaining a directive to your group, presenting an year end report and so on. The behaviour here should be autocratic. The information flow is from you to others, so participative

reactions are not needed here. You may accept suggestions, but in this situation you should be prepared to be firm or tough once a decision has been made.

3. **Decision making:** Situations covered here are planning a cost reduction program, setting up a work schedule, establishing a new pricing policy and so on. The behaviour style here should be participative. Every member of the group can contribute in making it a better decision. Also, participative management must exist, otherwise, you will need to be autocratic and tough, which can make people closed towards you.

4. **Problem Solving:** This includes solving customer problems, solving work flow breakdowns, handling urgent situations or crises and so on. Your behaviour here should encourage participation. This is necessary in order to use all the resources available for achieving the best results.

5. **Decision Selling:** These situations cover, getting employees to accept new organizational setups passed down by the board of directors, implementing changes in accounting practice, following up on decisions already made with the help of your work group and so on. Your behaviour here needs to be autocratic. You cannot afford distractions or delays, Firmness, and even toughness in such situations would be appreciated by the majority of your work group. However, you may switch to participative leadership for carrying out the decisions, because individual contributions and suggestions can be helpful at such a stage. However, any attempts by a small segment of the work group to change a decision already made, should be met with toughness.

Managers who have been firm and tough in their commitments have always gained results as well as employee admiration. Therefore, be prepared to get tough when necessary in order to get the best results from your people.

But people tend to resist change. In the next chapter, lets understand how to minimise resistance to change.

Chapter 4

HOW TO MINIMIZE
RESISTANCE TO CHANGE

◎ The seating arrangements in an office need to be rearranged to accommodate three new employees.

◎ As a result of the studies made by the industrial engineering department, the operator of a paper coating machine is required to operate two new coating machines simultaneously, instead of operating one old paper coating machine, as had been the custom.

◎ A sales manager is told by the sales director that in view of the new marketing strategy adopted by the company, within three months he should retrain and reassign salesmen on a region-wise basis, rather than on the existing product-wise basis.

◎ The purchasing manager of a plant is asked by the plant manager to introduce the changes in the inventory control system as advised by a firm of management consultants.

◎ The general manager of a sewing machine factory announces that as a part of the drive to improve the profitability of the factory's operations, a fresh evaluation of the production bonus scheme is to be made in order to set up new production and wastage standards.

◎ The board of directors of a company decides to diversify the organization's principle business activities by entering the field of office equipment.

These and many other similar situations are examples of the numerous changes which managers are required to deal with and implement. If you were the manager who was asked to implement some of these changes, you would find a number of similarities in each one of them. Each of these instances relates to the introduction of change, the need for which arises from the desire to achieve improvements and benefits.

All such changes invariably involve and affect people. In every case, the benefits and improvements are dependent on the behaviour of both the managers and the people affected. Even though change is a fact of life and is often very desirable, individuals and groups have a natural tendency to resist change unless it is clearly and assuredly for the better. Changes tend to generate feelings of uncertainty and doubt among those involved. As most managerial decisions involve some change, whether it be minor or major, temporary or permanent, this resistance becomes a common problem which the manager consciously or involuntarily has to face in the organization setting. Therefore, in dealing with and managing people successfully, it becomes important to understand how to minimize their resistance to desirable and necessary changes.

Understanding Why People Fear Change

All individuals need security. Security comes from a familiar and unchanging environment. Therefore, each individual is apprehensive of change and tends to resist it to protect his known status.

The basic causes for resistance are both the imagined and real effects of the change, together with the manner in which it is being brought about. Actually the change is often only the symbol of what is being opposed. It is necessary to get a clear understanding of why people fear change before one can take effective steps to minimize their resistance to change.

An individual's apprehensions are based upon attitudes which result from seven interrelating factors:

1. **A predisposed feeling about change**

   Different people react differently to change. Some individuals are suspicious and distrustful. Others are self-confident and approach change with objective questions based on the realities of the situation. One can deal with such reactions from different people if one understands what causes their attitudes to be different.

   Right from childhood we face changes which we naturally tend to resist. Take a lollipop away from a child and the result would be a scream of protest. Even a promise of two lollipops an hour later will not placate him. He wants immediate gratification. The memories of unpleasant childhood experiences and of the associated feelings of resistance, suspicion and distrust tend to persist during adulthood.

All adults have gone through some unpleasant childhood experiences. Nevertheless, the attitude of each adult tends to vary widely. This is because each individual has been handled differently by his parents and has different inherited strengths and weaknesses. A child who was forced to conform to unreasonable demands by unyielding parents will tend to regard almost every change with suspicion and fear. These feelings would tend to persist throughout his life. Such an adult would react to a change with unrelated personal fears and questions. You would not gain very much by using logical explanations and arguments with such an individual. You can minimize his resistance only by assuring him that he would not be harmed by the change; you are likely to get his cooperation and support as well.

On the other hand, a child whose parents were patient, flexible and understanding, would as an adult, regard change in a more favourable way. He would also question change, but in an objective and realistic manner. With such people it is only necessary to explain the need and usefulness of the change to get the necessary support and acceptance.

2. **Feelings of insecurity**
   Feelings of security or of insecurity result from an individual's cumulative experiences since birth, and become a part of his personality. They also reflect to a limited extent an individual's financial situation. Clearly, anyone with independent means is less likely to fear change affecting his job than a person who relies solely on his wage earnings.

   Such feelings have a deep impact on many aspects of human behaviour. They can cause a person to have fears without objective, logical justification. Such a person would find more reasons for objecting to a proposed change than would someone who felt more secure. Secure or insecure feelings also affect his self-confidence, resourcefulness and initiative. Finally, they determine how flexible and adaptable one is.

   If you are able to recognize illogical and unrealistic fears, you can then take appropriate steps to generate trust and confidence in the individuals concerned. You can assure them about how the change is likely to affect them.

3. Cultural beliefs and norms

All of us operate within numerous different socio-cultural set ups. These are the work group, the department or division of the organization, the organization as a whole, the community, the region, the nation and so on. Each of these societies has identifiable social & cultural beliefs and behavioural norms which influence individual attitudes towards change. In any business, as well as in its sub-divisions, there are cultural viewpoints concerned with the value of perpetuating certain practices. As in primitive societies, these viewpoints / beliefs are accepted implicitly, and are rarely, if ever, questioned.

For instance in some businesses:
◎ Skilled craftsman must have 'mates' or helpers to assist them.
◎ Long services / staying with a single organization is basically desirable.
◎ Perquisites should be proportional to the status of the job.
◎ The length of an employee's service in an organization should determine his rights to tenure, benefits and advancement.

Such cultural beliefs should not be labeled good or bad per se, but perceived in the context of the local environment. They depend on the motivations of the different societies interacting with one another in the organization setting. Treating them as being backward or irrelevant can generate tremendous resistance to management actions and changes. Whether good or bad, the prevailing cultural beliefs and behavioural norms become an important factor to be tackled by the manager in the event of a necessary change. Especially true when the cliques are pertinent to any change. This is illustrated by the following actual incident.

In a particular plant, skilled workers were given helpers to assist them. A change was introduced by the plant manager - the skilled workers stood to appreciably increase their earnings by foregoing the need for helpers. A few helpers with considerable experience were promoted to skilled workers and others were absorbed to fill certain vacancies and strengthen other sections. No one was retrenched. The plant manager was quite confident that his change would be welcomed, as it stood to benefit all concerned. It meant reduced expenses for the organization, higher earnings for the skilled workers, and a higher level or alternate employment to the helpers.

Nevertheless, the skilled workers, within a few days of the introduction of the change, organized a protest and gave a written notice through their union of a tool down strike unless the old system was reinstated. The plant manager, by introducing the change without considering the feelings of the skilled workers, had overlooked the significance of the value which each skilled worker attached to his social status in doing only skilled work and having a helper. This value was far greater to him than the additional income which was promised as a result of the change. The skilled workers implicitly believed that they should not perform any work which is outside the boundaries of their craft.

The management had to revert back to the previous system to keep the plant from closing down. They could introduce the change only after about a year, by which time they were able to change the value attached by skilled workers to having helpers. The attitude change was brought about by emphasizing the dignity attached to labor and self-help, and by citing examples of other plants and organizations where the proposed system was working well.

Therefore, one must be aware of both the existence and the potential significance of the cultural beliefs and norms prevalent in your organization and its subdivisions. With this knowledge, you would be able to recognize when a specific change is in conflict with one or more of these cultural beliefs and norms. This would put you in a better position to understand and minimize, if not avoid, such conflicts. Sometimes despite your best efforts, conflicts occur. This is not the time to fret. Having recognized the possibility of a conflict you can:

☞ Change the conflicting cultural belief and consequent attitudes.
☞ Modify the proposed change so that it does not conflict with cultural values.
☞ Adapt both the proposed change and the cultural values to suit each other as far as possible. The specific action which you take would vary with every situation.

4. **Trust in management, union and work groups.**
    Another factor that influences an individual's attitudes towards change is the nature of his relationships with others, either in the management or subgroups in the organization. If one has considerable trust in his leader, he would probably have faith that whatever the change, his welfare will be looked after. On the other hand, if there is little trust, he would be fearful of a proposed change. Similarly, if he lacks confidence in his union and his workmates, he would be inwardly even more opposed to a change, as he would tend to feel that his future security depended primarily on his own ability to protect his interests.

Loyalty and trust for the company, the manager and the union are developed through a series of direct personal experiences and observations.

These are also influenced by the existing cultural beliefs. Thus, it is likely that most individuals would conform to the prevailing cultural beliefs about the insincerity and general untrustworthiness of an organization's management.

The manager must accept that if there is little trust, his problems of implementing change will be difficult. He can attempt to counterbalance a lack of trust situation by providing explicit and firm facts and guarantees, and by a gradual introduction of change through a series of experimental trials. In situations where the manager has built up considerable trust between himself and his work group, resistance to change would tend to be far less than what might otherwise be and acceptance would follow.

5. **Historical events relevant to the change.**
    An individual's attitudes toward change are also influenced by the historical events relevant to the change. Thus, an organization's past policies, practises & customs, the extent to which the management has proved themselves trustworthy, the manner in which past changes have been carried out - all become examples of relevant historical events in the organization that influence people and determine their reactions to future changes.

    People often regard past events as precedents for what is likely to occur in the future. It's therefore advantageous for the manager to take into account past historical events relevant to a proposed change. With such knowledge, he can counterbalance the influence of those historical events which might have had a potentially negative effect on the group / person's attitude. Conversely, one can use advantageously those past happenings that might have had a beneficial effect on attitudes towards a change.

6. **Expectations and apprehensions about a particular change.**
    An organization has its own needs. The most compelling need is to survive in a state of homeostatic equilibrium with its environment. Thus, the need arises for improvement in products, sales volume, public image, human relations and so on. Most changes introduced by

managers are aimed at meeting these ends. Such changes can, however, bring into sharp focus, conflicts between both the immediate and long-term needs of the organization and those of the people involved. On the other hand, sometimes these needs will be more in harmony than in conflict. In any case, change tends to arouse apprehensions as well as expectations among those involved. A manager must be able to cope with the conflicts and questions which a change poses for different individuals. Some questions that an individual may ask about the proposed change are:

◎ How effective will I be in the new setup?
◎ Will the new situation mean more responsibility for me? Will I receive increased recognition?
◎ They are asking me to do something entirely different. Can it be done?
◎ In terms of the change, how will others regard me? What will be my status in their eyes?
◎ In the new situation, can my future performance be judged fairly? How will it be judged?
◎ What will my subordinates think of me? Will they alter their regard for me?
◎ How will customers, vendors and those outside the company react to me after the change? Will they consider this as an increase or decrease in my status in the company?
◎ How will my chances for advancement be affected?
◎ How important is the new situation for the company?
◎ How much is at stake on how good a job I do?

Many such questions will concern individual expectations.
Others may not be realistically based, such as those that stem from a feeling of insecurity. Whatever the nature of the questions, the manager will have to face them. As long as the individuals involved think of these as genuine problems, they must be dealt with by the manager. It is therefore important that the manager prepares himself to answer questions regarding individual and group expectations. Failure to do so will enhance individual fears and increase resistance to the change.

7.   **The manner of change.**
The manner in which a change is introduced and implemented also influences the attitudes of those involved in it. Whenever the management formulates a change, the number of orders given to subordinates tends to increase substantially. In such circumstances, people tend to lose their feelings of autonomy and self-sufficiency.

Their resentment of the change becomes heightened if the orders for the change appear to be arbitrary and unilateral. When people feel that they must alter their behaviour without any apparent reason, they are likely to be more stubborn in their opposition. Furthermore, if the change is presented as being irreversible and irrevocable; the groups suspicions and fears will inevitably increase. Insufficient information about the reasons for the change and its implications adds to definite fears about it. And when the mind is filled with questions which remain unanswered, any person is likely to invent answers. These self answers are often based on unnecessary imaginings and uncertainties resulting in an individual becoming even more suspicious and fearful of the change than he might have been otherwise.

When an employee is not treated as an individual, but merely as a member of a group, he resents the apparent lack of concern for his individual problems. This resentment is channelised into negative and resistant feelings toward the change. It has been repeatedly found that whenever a superior conveys to his subordinates a feeling of confidence in them, and an interest in their individual on-the-job and off-the-job problems, he is able to very positively motivate them towards achieving performance goals.

8. **Timing of the Change.**
Finally, the timing of a change can cause tensions. When sufficient time is not allowed for adjustment, those involved in a change develop apprehensions about their ability to cope with the new requirements. On the other hand, suitable timing for change introduction can often be used to help allay the fears of the those concerned.

Dinesh, the new manager of the distribution department of a large corporation, had completed a major study of its distribution operations. If certain improvements were made in the methods of operation, the company would be able to distribute its products with about 800 fewer employees. The company had been subcontracting many of its distribution operations. Dinesh's study showed that it would be economical to directly handle about three-fourths of the total distribution activities. The contracts with most of the subcontracting firms were coming up for renegotiation in a few months. The manager decided to time the improvement in distribution operations to coincide with the break points in these contracts. Thus, most of the employees who would have been over staff could be retained by re-absorption of the work being subcontracted.

When delaying the implementation of a desirable change, the manager must remember that it should not be for an indefinite period and must always be clearly beneficial when compared with the disadvantage of its immediate implementation. In the above example, the manager timed the controversial change with a reinforcing event in the near future to avoid the fear of an active resistance which would have otherwise resulted. Moreover the time before a change is actually implemented is critical. It should be used to help others understand the need for change.

Helping Others Understand The Need For Change

We have seen what factors influence an individual's fear of change. The manager can exert varying degrees of control over the influence of these factors. However, a manager has full control over only two factors. One of these is the extent of conflict between the interests of the people involved and those of the organization are rationalized. The other is the manner in which the change is introduced and implemented. Before getting into how to introduce and implement change, let us consider how those involved can best to be made to understand the need for change.

There are two methods used in practice. These help those involved to understand the need for and implications of a proposed change -
1. discussions to foster understanding 2. involvement and participation.

1. Discussions and Understanding

When the people involved in a change understand as much as possible about it and its consequences, their resistance is likely to be reduced. It is up to the manager to develop this understanding. Here, one should always make use of face to face discussions both with individuals and with groups. This is the most effective technique for ensuring that answers are given to questions of genuine concern from the employees involved. Additionally, this is the most effective means of determining how much real understanding is being achieved. The importance of creating real understanding through discussions with all concerned is illustrated in the following example:

A manager was temporarily successful in selling a change based on a complicated mathematical formula to a foreman who really did not understand it. It backfired, however, when the foreman tried to sell it to his operating people. He could not answer a number of sharp questions that they asked him. His embarrassment about this led him to resent and resist the change, so that eventually the whole idea fell flat. The manager was perplexed at the apparent change of heart in the foreman, and could not understand his dogged resistance to the change, especially since the foreman was one of the best in the plant. This was unfortunate not only in terms of human relations, but of technological progress in the plant as well.

Face to face discussion at planned intervals not only helps in conveying the need for a change to those involved and in answering their questions, but also gives feedback as to what problems are likely to arise due to the implementation of the changes.

To create the desired understanding of the change, the manager can additionally communicate the details of the change in writing through notices, circular, posters, articles, etc., or orally through announcements, formal orientation, etc. The more complex the change, the greater should be the variety of media employed.

2. **Involvement and Participation**
    Experience shows that when the people to be affected by a change are involved in its planning and implementation, they tend to understand and accept the need for change much better. The process of participation is a method of managing based on both, face to face discussions and involvement.

    The concept of using participation to generate understanding and acceptance among employees had become rather fashionable in management circles, but is quite loosely understood. The objective of a participative approach is to achieve acceptance by a group of people, in the sense that they are taking part in planning, initiating and implementing a change, instead of being merely the recipients of its effects. In practise, however, participation has come to mean different things to different employers. To some, it is a device for masterminding people to share the viewpoint held by the manager. To others it is a ritual to be observed so that there is an illusion created that the employees have some voice in what is going on and in what is happening to them. Such views are quite different from the true meaning of participation. Participation must truly and basically be a means for the manager to exercise his responsibility to the people who work with him, in order to provide them a sense of belonging based on human dignity. True participation cannot be created by management becoming an instruction agent. The art of assembling a group of people for discussion does not mean participation has been generated or is being motivated. Furthermore, it is not correct to assume that under all circumstances employees would want to participate. Studies of some business organizations have shown that in certain work groups, the need to be involved in the planning and implementation of desirable changes is absent or subordinated to other more pressing needs, such as job security.

When and how, then, can a manager ensure and use true participation? The following are the basic prerequisites / conditions that must be met (completely) for experiencing real participation :
The employees involved must want to participate.
- ☞ The manager must feel secure in his position so as to invite suggestions and participation from his subordinates.
- ☞ The manager must not be committed to any one course of action. He must be open-minded to possible alternative approaches for bringing about the desired change.
- ☞ The manager must be openly willing to give credit and recognition to all who make contributions of merit in regard to the change.
- ☞ The employees must be willing to voice their comments and to offer suggestions. Mere acceptance will not work with people who are passive and apathetic.

If all these conditions are not present, one would do well to be cautious in the use of participation as a management technique for generating understanding and acceptance of upcoming changes. He would profit in such situations by using face to face discussions to answer questions and clarify the need for change. Wherever feasible, he should use individual or group consultation to generate a fuller understanding of the problem that a change is expected to solve. Employee consultation is based on the correct, practical consideration that the man actually doing a job on a day-to-day basis, is usually more knowledgeable about it than anyone else. For instance;

The manager of an auto-accessories plant was facing an unusually stubborn problem. Product quality had fallen way-off, and none of the engineering staff was able to find a solution. Expensive consultants also failed to stop the increased flow of rejects. The manager had become conscious of his tendency to run the plant without employee consultation or participation. He decided to change his tactics to crack this tough problem, and asked for ideas and suggestions from his employees in a plant-wide meeting. After a painful silence, during which the "yes" men were looking around for someone to speak up, two individuals, generally viewed as incompetent, quietly but definitely took the problem apart, brought out the true causes, and laid out the solution. The manager listened to them with amazement and appreciation. He had not even known the capabilities of these men before he decided to change his approach and get them involved in running of the plant through the process of consultation.

In the process of consultation, the manager may accept or reject suggestions on their merit and worth. However, if an employee's suggestion is rejected, he must be made to understand why. Then consultation can still be very productive, even if the employees' suggestions need to be rejected. There are three reasons for this. First, the fact that an employee has an opportunity to express himself and be given serious attention is very beneficial to his attitude and morale. Also, by understanding why his suggestion is not acceptable, the employee can reach a better understanding of the change. Finally, he may be encouraged to offer better suggestions for the future.

If participation is to operate at a deeper level (where all the necessary conditions exist), it should involve the concerned employees in diagnosing the particular problems underlying the need for a change. The benefits of doing this are illustrated in the following case:

The manager of a plant manufacturing a wide variety of consumer products felt that the workers had developed negative attitudes about their jobs due to poor supervisory practises. He called a meeting of supervisors to tackle this problem, and set up a method incorporating their suggestions for diagnosing the cause of these negative attitudes among his workers. Later, the supervisors were called to another meeting to report their findings. At the meeting, their enthusiasm for change in their own practises was high because they had participated in gathering the facts relevant to their problems. They did not hesitate to bring in changes and improvements in their own practises and objectives in order to remove the negative attitudes of their workers, because they had participated in diagnosing their own problem.

People will generally act constructively on the basis of information gathered by them, rather than on the basis of information gathered by others and conveyed to them.

You can effectively use face-to-face discussions, written and oral communication, employee involvement and participation in many different ways to help others understand the need for change.

How to Discuss Upcoming Changes in a Group

In the process of managing people, a manager often needs to discuss approaching changes with groups. If he can do this well, the changes can be successfully implemented. This, in turn, undoubtedly contributes to his overall success as a manager. There are five essential steps which, as a manager, you must take, to successfully discuss upcoming changes in groups:

1. **Understanding the change yourself.**

   Before a manager can discuss a change, he must first fully understand what is about to happen. He must be able to answer the following questions:
   - ◎ What is to be done and why?
   - ◎ What are the different ways in which it can be accomplished?
   - ◎ What will change as a consequence?

   If he doesn't know some of the answers, then he must get them from his boss and others concerned. After getting the answers to these questions, he will be able to distinguish the means from the ends.

   In most situations, it is the ends or objectives that are important. Both immediate and long range objectives must be noted. Provided that the means used are ethical and moral, it matters little which ones are employed. However, what matters is how well the desired long range objectives can be accomplished by different means under consideration.

   One must remain as flexible as possible in selecting or modifying the means for achieving the desired objectives. He can do this if he maintains a clear separation in his mind between the objectives and the various methods that may be used to accomplish these objectives. When such a distinction is blurred, the methods can themselves become the primary objectives. When this occurs, the manager can become so committed to a particular method that he loses both flexibility and objectivity, essential to the success of any change. To remain flexible and objective, the manager must not only separate the methods from the objectives, but must also remain open to incorporating worthwhile suggestions from the groups where the change is to be reflected and that might be discussing the approaching change.

This raises the question of how discussion groups should be formed.

2. **Forming discussion groups.**
The formation of discussion groups depends upon the particular organization setup and the nature of a proposed change. Every manager needs to form a group or groups from between his immediate subordinates to discuss an upcoming change. If you have a number of sections or departments reporting to you, then these discussion groups would naturally tend to be along the lines of sectional , departmental and organization committees, depending upon your position in the organization hierarchy. These committees could also serve as discussion groups for other similar changes. Generally, these committees or groups would also be responsible for implementing the change. How this is done will be a matter to be discussed.

In case the nature of the change is such that it affects other departments, then representatives of those departments should be invited to participate in the discussion group or groups.

Having decided on the group or groups where an upcoming change is to be discussed, the manager should call for a preliminary meeting in which all concerned individuals should be present. Depending upon whether the requirement for change is a sudden development or not, the manager should give sufficient background information to all group members. Once this is done, the employees concerned, would be better informed and thus increase the possibility of useful suggestions being made during the course of the discussion.

3. **Planning for the discussion.**
The manager must plan in advance what is to be discussed. For this he must do the following:
☞ Prepare to explain the upcoming change keeping the perspective of the employees concerned.
☞ Anticipate possible questions and objectives, as well as the extent of resistance likely to be offered by different individuals. Be well equipped to explain all questions however uncomfortable they might be. Thereby minimize anticipated resistance by clearing doubts and fears, giving required assurances.
☞ Consider the method or possible methods for implementing

the change and plan on improving these, based on any useful suggestions and comments made by his employees during the discussion.

☞ Decide how best he can point out the advantages and added incentives, if any, which the change would bring to the employees when it is successfully implemented.

☞ Having prepared himself for the discussion, the manager can then plan how he is going to conduct it.

4. **Conducting the discussion.**
It is best to have the initial discussion in a large group comprising all employees. If need be, the discussion can be continued in smaller groups formed on a sectional, departmental or interdepartmental basis, depending upon the nature of the change.

During the discussion, the manager should provide the necessary background about the reason and objectives of the change and how it is likely to affect those present. He can then discuss group incentives, if any, and the expected participation of all present in making and reviewing suggestions for improving the effectiveness of the change. The discussion of group incentives becomes really important for major changes. Research in the running of business operations has proven that group incentives, as well as employee participation in planning and implementing all significant changes, contribute greatly to dramatically increase the overall efficiency of an organization. Further in the book, I will share an instance of where this was actually done in an organization.

The manager should then go through the possible methods of implementing the change and invite questions & suggestions. In case the change is one that would be implemented over a considerable period of time, he should also discuss where suitable conditions exist, the means of continuing employee participation for improving the effectiveness of the change. This is often done by the formation of standing committees. These standing committees meet periodically to discuss suggestions submitted individually. They then propose ways to overcome problems and obstacles in the efficient implementation of the change. The manager should form the standing committees, if necessary, and allocate responsibilities for any follow-up that needs to be done. Throughout the discussion, the manager must allow ample opportunities for getting employee reactions, questions and suggestions.

Here is an actual example of how discussing an upcoming change in groups can bring amazing results.

The manager of a printing plant had tried to introduce a conveyor system. The design engineers had developed the plans without consulting any of the employees. From the very start, the system failed to work properly, and the employees showed no interest to make it work.

To generate interest in the employees, the manager decided to discuss the conveyor system afresh with them in a group. He had a small scale model of the proposed system layout made to provide the necessary background information for the employees at the time of the discussion. At the discussion meeting, after he had given the necessary details of what was expected from the new system and why, he encouraged those present to suggest improvements and speak their mind on the proposed change. Based on these comments which came forth, a joint production committee was formed which made modifications to eliminate problems the engineers had overlooked. The engineers were happy with the interest of the employees in the new system and cooperated to incorporate the useful suggestions they had received. Needless to say, the new system ran successfully and appreciably improved the plant productivity and the earnings of the employees.

The manager in the preceding example admitted that he had actually got the idea to discuss the new system with the employees concerned, in a management development seminar, where he learned about the **Scanlon Plan**. The **Scanlon plan** is named after the man who devised it, and is primarily a program with two basic elements:

i)   Participation of employees through group discussions, joint committees and so on, to improve the effectiveness of an operation or change.

ii) It involves some form of group incentive.

It is such an approach to managing people that it gears both the attitude and capability of all employees towards carrying out changes for improvement. A manager can use this approach to improve his overall operating effectiveness. There is no standard approach to the group incentive. Typically, it is a wage formula that provides every employee (sometimes even managers) to receive a monthly bonus based on monthly improvements in operating effectiveness. This is generally measured in terms of output to total payroll costs and is developed through discussions and negotiations either with the employees concerned or their union representatives. Once in operation, it also provides a feedback to the employees as to how well they are achieving their common desired objectives.

The great strength of an approach of this type rests with the participation of employees, which is achieved primarily through discussions in groups and committees formed at various levels in the organization. Suggestions affecting the organization as a whole are sent up to the organization level committee, comprising of members of top management and employee leadership. Notable suggestions are rewarded at each level. Suggestions are rejected only after careful consideration, and are accompanied by full explanations. This overall approach can work only if the manager can abandon traditional prerogatives and attitudes, and if, as discussed earlier, favourable conditions exist for participation. The experience of managers who have used this approach has shown that this has made possible the introduction of changes which the manager could not have introduced otherwise. Wherever used, this approach minimizes resistance to change since rather than imposing the change on people, it involves them in the process of creating that change.

A Systematic Approach To Making Changes

There is no standard method for making changes as no single approach can take into account the enormous variability of the factors present in every situation and organization. Secondly, there are different personal styles of leadership and this precludes the possibility of any single method. Nevertheless, it is possible that a manager can be helped to develop a systematic approach to the way he implements changes. There are certain essential considerations which a manager must take into account for successfully implementing a change, irrespective of the situation or organization he is in. These considerations can be looked upon as a personal checklist relevant to planning & implementing a desirable change.

The following five steps are essential for successfully realizing any change:

    I.   Analyzing and planning the change
    II.   Communicating the change
    III. Gaining acceptance
    IV. Making the initial transition
    V.   Consolidating and following up

I. Analyzing and planning the change

Indeed, the first step a manager should take for introducing any significant change is to develop a clear understanding of the change: its basis, objectives, scope and implications. We have already discussed how he can go about doing this.

Having understood the basis and nature of the proposed change, the manager can proceed to estimate its effects on those involved and their probable reactions. Based on his estimation of the difficulties and resistance that lie ahead, he can plan a program for minimizing them. One can do this by helping others understand the need for change and discussing it in groups. I reiterate that this procedure, discussed earlier, requires the manager to regard the change from the viewpoint of those likely to be affected by the change. The manager must plan to eliminate the many objectionable aspects of the change and as far as practical, provide rewards to offset objectionable aspects which cannot be eliminated.

Finally, one must develop a tentative but specific time plan for the introduction, implementation and follow up of the desired change. This can best be done first, by identifying and listing each distinct task for implementing the change. The dependent tasks must be separated from the independent ones. Thus, one will find that some tasks must be completed before others are begun, and some can be carried out at any time. These should be arranged in proper sequential and parallel relationships, and the time needed to complete each task should then be estimated. The highest priority should be given to completing those dependent tasks, which on further analysis are critical to the achievement of the overall change. A delay in any of these critical elements would cause a delay in the overall change. For simple changes, the manager can put down this plan in a simple, schematic form on a sheet of paper, which serves as his master plan of action and a means of controlling and comparing actual versus planned performance. For complex changes requiring many separate tasks or steps, the manager may use the techniques of network analysis (CPM or PERT) to develop a timed plan. This analysis may be done by the manager himself or, as is more generally the case, with the assistance of the project or staff department concerned.

The manager should involve his subordinates and key members of any relevant staff service groups in creating a timed plan for action and in planning a program for minimizing resistance. This involvement of the concerned and key personnel will ensure that the plan developed is realistic. It will also help in its implementation as it will become the commitment not only of the manager, but also of all those who participated in the planning process.

II. Communicating the change

The next step is to help everyone concerned understand the need for change through varied communication media. As discussed, these would include face-to-face discussions, employee involvement and participation, written communications and so on. At this stage, the manager would also have to deal with the union wherever pertinent.

From the leader's point of view, the purpose of this communication should be twofold - Firstly, he must ensure that all those involved get an understanding of the reasons for the change, its objectives, anticipated benefits, intended methods of approach and its proposed implementation schedule. Secondly, the manager should assess both individual and group reactions after their questions, beliefs and fears about the change are satisfactorily dealt with.

This can only be achieved by making communication a two way process. The manager must elicit comments and suggestions from the employees concerned. He must allow for sufficient discussion opportunities to communicate the rationale of the change and get the necessary feedback & suggestions from the employees. When a change is complex and has far reaching implications, the manager should plan his implementation schedule so that sufficient time is allowed for discussions and reassuring through communication.

Action to remove cultural barriers, mistaken notions and irrational fears can best be initiated during the communication phase of a change. This lays the necessary foundation for getting acceptance to any change.

III. Gaining acceptance to the method of change

A manager can get agreement on a particular method of change in various ways. He can offer rewards or use persuasion. Alternatively, he can negotiate and bargain with the representatives of the employees. Or he can encourage people to participate and arrive at the best mode of accomplishing the change. Moreover, the manager can use any combination of these approaches. The particular approach to be used would depend upon the circumstances of each situation.

Persuasion or rewards may be appropriate for situations where the manager is faced with only one particular method for effectively achieving the desired change. Negotiations and bargaining may be required to gain acceptance, especially if there is a union involved and the change is relevant to a labor agreement. Participation of the employees is most desirable when it is possible to achieve the change in a variety of ways. This participation invariably proves very rewarding, as it helps the manager to choose a method of implementation which causes the least resistance.

Whatever approach is used by the manager, he is likely to come across special personal problems from some of the employees concerned. The manager can overcome such problems by remaining sufficiently flexible in his attitude and approach. Exceptions and modifications to meet individual needs may be carried out to overcome genuine disparities which may be unfair to some employees. These will be accepted by the group if they understand and perceive the exceptions as reasonable.

The effectiveness of the approach taken generally depends upon how much discussion or constructive communication takes place. Discussions should begin at the start of the communication phase, and should continue until agreement is reached on how to proceed with the actual transition.

Once acceptance has been gained from most employees regarding the method of implementing the change, the manager can confidently get into the task of its actual implementation.

IV. Making the initial transition

At the start of the initial transition from the existing to the new condition, the manager should review the time planned for the change. He should consider whether it is desirable and possible to test the method of implementation on a trial basis. This can be done by either having a trial area or group, or by establishing a trial period. It is generally desirable to do this for complex changes where the outcomes cannot be realistically estimated. Such a trial provides an opportunity to test and experience the effects of the change, before it is made permanent. It can serve to modify the change and can help to implement it successfully in its new form. On the other hand, where there is clear desirability and acceptance of a change, the manager should implement the change in its entirety. Alternatives and improvements can always be made later or whenever desirable.

Once it is finalized how the transition is to take place, the leader has to see that everyone involved is briefed on what is to take place and who is to do what. The briefing should help the employees to establish what their roles will be during the transition period and in the new situation.

If the change requires new knowledge and skills, then training activities must be planned and carried out. This will not only help the employees to carry out their new responsibilities efficiently, but will also help to reduce any fears and doubts about their new responsibilities. This training, if warranted, should be imparted to all involved – right from the managerial to the operative or clerical levels. In case of complex changes, sufficient time must be scheduled for such trainings to be completed before the change is implemented.

Supervision has to be more thorough during the period of transition than otherwise. The manager must remain continually informed about what is happening at the scene of the change and what progress is being achieved. To obtain a constant flow of timely information, the manager should employ various means. He should have his supervisors report to him daily on the progress achieved and he should frequently discuss the situation with them. Staff specialists, if involved in the planning of the change, should be encouraged to contribute ideas, comments and assistance to its implementation. Where the union is involved, the progress should also be discussed with their representatives. Finally, and most importantly, the manager should pay frequent visits to the scene of action in order to gain first hand information about what is happening. During these visits, he should chat informally (with genuine concern) with those involved to get an overall assessment. This will enable him to take immediate corrective action, should that be necessary.

V. Consolidation and follow-up
The final phase in any change consists of the consolidation of the new conditions and also the follow-up of events after the initial transition has been made. This phase should be continued by the manager till the change meets success.

Even though the initial transition may have been accomplished smoothly, the manager should not presume the change itself has been successfully achieved. What may appear to be a successful implementation of the change at the outset may result in failure, due to the effects of subsequent factors. The manager can avoid this failure by consolidating the initial transition and by attending to problems & difficulties as they occur. He must remain flexible enough to institute desirable modifications in the way the change is being carried out.

As mentioned before, after the finishing touches have been given to the initial transition, the manager has to employ a number of means to consolidate and follow up on the change. The manager should institute a procedure whereby he receives regularly scheduled oral and written reports from his immediate subordinates and from staff specialists involved. These reports should compare the actual progress made and compare it to the planned schedule towards achieving the objectives of the change. The manager should supplement this reporting procedure with on-the-spot visits and interviews with all directly involved in the change.

The manager's own first-hand knowledge, combined with the regular reports he receives, will enable him to evaluate the extent to which the anticipated benefits and results have been achieved. If the objectives have been clearly defined, this comparison becomes both easy and informative. Such a follow-up procedure will reveal the existence of additional problems if they do exist. The manager can thereby act swiftly to either initiate further detailed investigations into the areas of difficulty, or to modify the appropriate elements of the change.

By following such a systematic approach to making changes, you will be able to minimize people's resistance to change. It will become an important aid to managing people successfully and getting them to say "Yes" not just in oral agreement but in principle.

We all come across problem people and need to know how to deal with them. The following chapter, will share some effective ways to manage problem people.

Chapter - 5

HOW TO MANAGE PROBLEM PEOPLE

Every manager gets his share of problem people. These are people who do not perform their job in a satisfactory manner and impede the achievement of organization objectives.

Being able to recognize such people and deal with them effectively can help you to appreciably improve the overall performance of your work team. Progressive managers today, are directing their efforts more and more towards developing the problem employee, and helping him to become a satisfactory and desirable member of a work team. But before one can solve a problem efficiently, one must understand it fully. Thus, before you can successfully manage problem people, you need to know who they are and why they behave as they do.

Identifying Problem People

All problem people in an organization can be categorized into one of the following three categories:
1. Those who do not perform satisfactorily.
2. Those who are non-cooperative and impede team work.
3. Those who break organization rules and codes of ethics in a severe and /or consistent manner.

The reason why problem people do not perform, are non-cooperative or break rules is worth analyzing. The egos of some people drive them to do individualistic and detrimental activity. Such individuals tend to be non-cooperative. Mental slowness and sheer laziness can be other causes of people becoming problematic. Lastly, insufficient background, skill or education, or an unhealthy attitude towards work, can make an employee a problem case.

You can categorize your problem people in the three groups mentioned above. For each problem employee so categorized, you can then analyze the reasons which contribute to his problem behaviour. These may be his ego, mental lethargy, laziness, insufficient background and skill, improper job assistance, work attitude, unsuitable ill health, financial debt, bad personal habits and so on. Once you have thought through who your problem people are and what some of the reasons for their unsatisfactory behaviour are, you can plan to deal with them effectively. A key factor in handling existing or potentially problem people is to encourage them to freely discuss problems.

Encouraging People To Discuss Problems Freely

Countless number of employees could have been saved from becoming organizational burdens, had their manager been open to listening to their problems. Therefore, both as a cure and a preventive measure, you have to encourage your work group to discuss problems freely amongst themselves and with you. However this is easier said than done. You can encourage people to air their problems by taking the following steps:

1. **Keep an open door policy.** Many managers think that they maintain an open door policy, but reality their subordinates are either afraid or think it not worthwhile to discuss their problems with the boss, as they know nothing beneficial will result from it. An open door policy is practical and will work only if the manager keeps an open mind, too. This means not criticizing or prejudging what others have to convey. It also means not passing the buck, and doing something constructive wherever possible to set a problem situation right. An example will serve to illustrate how one manager implemented an open door policy, and saw to it that it worked.

    A well reputed organization's top management advocated an open door policy for all employees. Each manager was encouraged to hear out and make it possible for any employee in his work group to communicate freely with him. Though this policy existed on paper, very few managers were really regarded as being open to employee problems. Others merely gave lip service to the policy. Rohit Kapoor was one of the managers reputed to manage his people efficiently. His subordinates could communicate freely with him, and he had been known to make good workers out of people who had caused problems in other assignments. In fact, some problem people from other departments had been transferred to his department, and had been performing well since. Rohit took the policy of keeping an open door to employee problems and suggestions. In order to encourage people to discuss their problems freely, he had a brief department meeting at the beginning of every month. This was an open forum where anyone could voice a suggestion and bring up a problem for group solution. Some months the meeting lasted only 15 minutes. Other months it went up to two hours. Rohit also used the opportunity provided by the meeting to voice his own thoughts about the departmental performance, how it was doing, and what required a little more emphasis in the coming month. All his subordinates knew that they could air their difficulties and problems at such meetings. Nevertheless, there are always some employees who hesitate to express themselves in front of a group. Rohit encouraged his people to discuss their problem individually with him too. To avoid time wasting sessions, he asked his people to come prepared with relevant facts and figures, wherever applicable, when they wanted to discuss a problem. He fully heard every person who came to him without interruption. He had learnt that a premature response to cut short an employee who had not finished all that he had to say often left the employee dissatisfied. Rohit took the time to counsel unsatisfactory or marginal performers on how they could improve their work. Quite often, hearing them out made it clear that they needed to be assigned to some other responsibility, in which they had greater interest and proficiency. More importantly, he had a cardinal rule with regards to discussing problems - something would be done about it. This motivated his people to discuss problems freely with him, thereby assisting him in managing them better. This was reflected in the high grade of work accomplishment achieved by his department.

An open door policy toward employees must be adopted to suit your own particular situation. It should not only be existent in name, but in practice as well.

2. **Encourage Group Discussions:** Another excellent means of getting people to discuss problems freely is to provide such a forum in group meetings. These meetings may be called occasionally to discuss a particular organization situation or may be called on a regular basis for reviewing performance and discussing problems faced by individuals or subgroups. Such discussions tend to increase cooperation amongst the group and make the group more effective.

Let us see how providing an opportunity to discuss a critical problem freely in a group, helped a manager to handle a difficult situation effectively.

Girish managed the sales department of a machine tools factory. He had problems in retaining his people. Most of those who did not leave had become problems in themselves, as they did not perform well. The efficiency of the sales department was low indeed. Girish knew from different individuals in his work team that they did not get the necessary support from the design and production department to meet customers' changing requests and be competitive in the market. The production and design departments went strictly by the rules, and sometimes Girish had to go to the general manager to get their cooperation. On the other hand, the production and design departments had a few bones to pick with sales and felt that they did not understand technical limitations and were non-cooperative. Employees on both sides were becoming thick-skinned. The sales force was not motivated to stretch itself to increase sales. Girish discussed this unhappy situation at length with his boss, the general manager. They agreed that it was necessary to establish a special forum for free discussion of mutual problems on an interdepartmental basis, every month. Girish complemented this move in his department by having weekly work group meetings to provide opportunity for a frank discussion on operating problems and critical situations. People who were becoming frustrated and tired of the existing situation voiced their feelings openly in these weekly meetings. Group discussions helped to increase mutual understanding, and a number of minor problems were resolved through ideas brought out during these discussions. After a few weeks of these discussion forums, Girish's work group suggested a change in order taking procedure and the input provided for production planning. Interestingly, some of the poor performers had some very good suggestions which were matured in the group discussions and put into effect in a practical manner. One of the suggestions that was immediately implemented was for all in the sales force to receive special training in the factory. This helped sales to understand the technical capacities of the factory for different products and to know what last minute changes were possible and which were not.

As a result of the interdepartmental monthly discussions, a new sales ordering and production planning procedure was jointly arrived at, alleviating the difficult and frustrating situation which had developed over time. The group meetings were continued, because their usefulness as a forum discussing operating problems freely had been established. In his work group meetings, Girish did not leave it up to the outspoken employees alone to dominate the discussions, which is generally the case. He asked each employee, by name, if they had anything to say. This ensured that even the more subdued and reticent employees were encouraged to discuss their problems.

3. **Utilizing T-Group Sessions:** Establishing a practical means of encouraging people to discuss problems freely, on an interdepartmental and work group basis, had helped to change organization and work group basis and the organization's problem people into members of an efficient, cooperative endeavour. Appropriate group discussions can be very important in reducing organization frustrations of employees. A somewhat related means of encouraging people to discuss interpersonal problems freely is through their participation in T-group sessions. Utilize

T-group sessions wherever possible. These are sensitivity training sessions. This is very successful, modern approach to work group and individual development. The purpose is to establish a free means of communication between the people taking part in the sessions, so that they can understand themselves and others better. The result is an increased sensitivity and appreciation of interpersonal relationships in the work situation. Problems are thereby thoroughly discussed in the proper perspective, and in a frank and free manner

The benefits of T-group sessions are manifold. They serve to:
(i)   initiate individual employee development
(ii)   develop cooperative behaviour
(iii) bring interpersonal problems to light, and
(iv) help change problem people.

In chapter 4, we saw how an organisation took advantage of the opportunity to have T-group sessions for his work team. These sessions clearly resulted in developing cooperative light. That was the express purpose of having the sensitivity training session to help develop employees both individually and as a group. Let us see how these sessions helped some problem employees to discuss their feelings openly and overcome their handicaps.

Jatin managed the industrial relations and personnel department of an organization manufacturing electronic components and products. Though he had been careful to get suitable personnel for his department, he knew that most of them needed to develop themselves individually to handle their jobs better. In fact, he considered some of them as 'problem' employees since they got tongue-tied in difficult situations and became completely ineffective, He wanted to increase the sensitivity of his people to interpersonal problems and further develop their ability to explain and discuss various issues with outsiders, union representatives and corporate employees. Sometimes problems were created when his staff had dealt with a situation tactlessly or when in his absence, one of his people couldn't explain an aspect of personnel policy to an irate employee.

Jatin had heard of sensitivity training as a means of making people sensitive to their individual developmental needs. He got in touch with a management consultant who had conducted sensitivity training sessions, to find out if they could be arranged for the employees of his department. Although the work group sessions were a new development, he was happy to know that they could be arranged. It was decided to have three sessions, once a week, for about four weeks.

The first meeting was disappointing. Employees were expecting programmed

instructions, but found none. They were told that all meetings would be informal and that they should suggest their own subjects or topics of common interest to discuss. Furthermore, anyone could initiate a discussion by group agreement. The management consultant defined his role merely as an observer and coordinator of the sessions. There was very little discussion as such in the first session. Some employees said that all this seemed to be a gross waste of time.

In the second session, a poll was taken by the group as to what topics should be discussed. Out of frustration and possible feeling of getting it over with, the employees suggested a wide variety of subjects ranging from politics to employee benefits. The group's majority rejected some topics and allowed discussions to be held on a few topics. This included discussion on problems faced by individuals on a day to day basis.

The management consultant seemed to be passive and let the group go the way it wanted. Some active members in the group dominated the discussions. After a while, however, the quiet members of the group were asked by one of the supervisors to express their viewpoints as well.

In the third session, the supervisor allowed discussions on organizational topics of common interest to continue for about an hour. Then the management consultant distributed a general knowledge quiz, first to be completed individually and then to be tackled in a group. The group effort produced a higher score than any individual score in the group. In another subgroup, it was found that two individuals had higher scores than the group score. Obviously, the first subgroup had demonstrated better team work than the second. This exercise helped to highlight some of the problems in group cooperation and maximization of effort. Some individuals were surprised to see other colleagues do better than they were expected to.

The last session was devoted to an analysis of the demonstrated strengths and weaknesses of each individual. First, a general list of desirable strengths and undesirable shortcomings, relative to the department needs, was made. Then, one by one, every employee was discussed. By this time, a rapport had been established and everyone was beginning to see how a group review would help him to plan his own development. Against every individual's name, the group was asked to express what they felt were his strengths and weaknesses. Then the individual concerned was asked to express what he felt were his strong and weak points. This helped each individual compare how others saw him with what he thought of himself. This understanding of how others perceive you and how you perceive yourself is very important. It was effectively brought out through this excercise. Most employees found the last *session rather illuminating. Each employee now somewhat understood the feelings he aroused in others and why. This list of projected strengths and weaknesses helped each individual to see the need for improvement and the area where it was needed.*

These sessions in themselves helped to change a few individuals appreciably for the better. There was one employee who had never discovered for himself that he could lead a group discussion. In the course of these sessions, he had been asked to do so. He was certainly a changed individual. He had developed the self-confidence to express himself during these sessions, whereas earlier he had always doubted his own capability to do that. Another interesting effect was that employees now felt that they knew each other much more intimately than before. The result was that interpersonal problems were discussed more freely and that made the department more effective in its organizational role. Jatin had successfully utilized T-group sessions to initiate the development of his people and give them the confidence and understanding to discuss problems freely.

Depending on your organizational situation, you can use Keeping an open door policy, Encouraging group discussions, and Utilizing T-group sessions in any suitable combination to encourage your people to discuss problems without hesitation.

Day-to-day Dealing With Problem People

The biggest hurdle in dealing with problem people is emotion. The problem person is often an emotionally ridden individual who will generate emotions in you as well - generally of a negative nature. You will have to control your feelings before you can handle him effectively. Experience has shown that you can profit by following a four steps approach in dealing with problem people:

1. **Control your emotions:** Problem people were not always like that. Very often, problem people are created by the force of negative emotions from other people. Good behaviour begets good behaviour. Never resign an employee permanently to the 'problem' category. Approach every situation without bias. Give problem people opportunities to change for the better in order to get the recognition or esteem they desire. Do not try to hurt their ego - problem people are overly sensitive to matters of pride. On the other hand, do not pretend to be too nice or considerate, either. Most people do not like charitable behaviour towards them. They like to believe that what they have is because of their own strengths and not a favour handed over in a platter.

2. **Give importance to individual feelings:** No one can confidently introduce a desirable change in a person without understanding what his emotional needs are. Therefore, the emotions / feelings of the right-now-problem person are important if you want to change his behaviour. This can be done by looking at the situation from his point of view, rather than your own. Then only can you appeal to what is important enough to him to change his behaviour for the better.

3. **Learn the other's side of the story:** In addition to understanding the concerned person's emotions it is necessary to learn about his work constraints and day to day operational problems.

4. **Get mutual agreement on principles of revised behaviour:** The next step is to get mutual agreement on improved behaviour and performance. This mutual agreement may be either implied or clearly spelled out depending upon the situation. In the case of ego or insufficient background cases, it may be preferable to simply imply the principles of revised behaviour. Nevertheless, in the cases of lethargy or laziness, it is generally better to mutually and clearly, spell out rules of acceptable behaviour and performance.

Let us see how a very successful manager followed these four steps in dealing with problem people in his particular situation.

The marketing manager of a gas range company was unsuccessful in persuading the production manager to make certain modifications in the standard product. These changes were important so that he could win an order from an apartment builder for providing built-in cooking ranges. Even in the past, the production manager had been reluctant to accept any order except the ones for the standard models or for very large volume non-standard items. His rigid approach had become quite a problem. The marketing manager knew that the apartment builder's order was non-standard and small. Nevertheless, he saw that this would mean a large future order from the builder if this time he was given the product modifications he wanted. The marketing manager wanted to avoid going to the Vice President in charge of operations to get the order accepted, as that would further worsen the work relationship between him and the production manager. He decided to control his own emotions and re-assess the situation with the production manager. He made arrangements that a joint meeting with the builder's representative be held. He felt that this would enable the production manager to explain what could or couldn't be done. He stated that the production manager would be able to do a better job of this than he could hope to do by himself. Because he appealed to the production manager's self-esteem, he got agreement for such a meeting. The production manager suggested that the engineering manager be there as well. The marketing manager was glad to arrange that.

The marketing manager hoped that the production and engineering manager would be able to persuade the apartment builder's project manager to accept one of the standard models. Alternatively, he hoped that the prospective customer would convince the production manager to take the job.

As it turned out, the two technical managers persuaded the customer to drop several of the more troublesome modifications and agreed to incorporate the less difficult change. The marketing manager had finally learnt the way to change the behaviour of the production manager. He regularized a procedure whereby he met the esteem needs of the production manager by encouraging his direct interaction with the customer for all non-standard product orders.

In the above example, the marketing manager dealt with his problem person, the production manager, by (1) controlling his own emotions, (2) understanding the esteem needs of the production manager, (3) allowing for operational difficulties, and (4) establishing an acceptable approach to handling order requests for non-standard items by introducing the practice of joined consultation with the customer.

This four step approach is very helpful when dealing with problem people / problem subordinates who do not follow desirable forms of organizational behaviour. The fourth step, in such cases, would mean establishing organizational rules to limit or discourage undesirable behaviour. Thus, to avoid drinking, hazardous smoking, insubordination and so on, it is best to formulate clear-cut rules, if they do not exist already. When some employees choose to violate rules, one can impose penalties that are commensurate with the situation. They may range from a warning to a discharge. If there is a union contract, then ofcourse, the matter has to be dealt with through established channels. The significant thing to remember is that no matter what the rule, it must be uniformly and consistently applied; otherwise, even though an employee may be a clear violator, undesirable results may follow attempted enforcement.

A troublesome employee, who was discharged after being late for the twelfth time (under a company rule providing for discharge should an employee be late 12 times in a year), had to be reinstated with back pay and seniority rights. The arbitrator called the rule arbitrary and unreasonable, in view of a past practice of remitting up to 36 late arrivals a year and a system of warning, now abandoned.

In addition to the danger of being challenged, a rule which is haphazardly or inconsistently applied will confuse employees, rather than curb undesirable behaviour. It is essential therefore to see that rules are enforced in a consistent manner. Experience has shown that when dealing with instances of rule violations, formal written warnings bolster disciplinary system in several ways:

The significance of the offense is brought home. There is a powerful psychological effect in a formal written warning. It provides official recognition by the management, of the importance of undesirable behaviour.

Consistent and fair enforcement is emphasized. An employee cannot claim that a supervisor is unfair if he is shown that similar warnings have been sent to other employees in the past, wherever applicable. A better rating of the employee is made possible. A complete record of warnings helps to rate employees with reduced uncertainty. There is greater likelihood of legal approval. Arbitrators and law courts will more readily uphold a decision if the records show that the employee had received previous warning. A violator is often let off with a reduced penalty, if he has not been warned. Though formal arbitration applies only to unionized businesses, the general approach in handling difficult personal problems discussed here is equally desirable for non-union organizations as well.
?
Rererring Serious Difficulties to Helpful Experts

Sometimes the four-step approach, discussed above, to deal with problem people on a day to day basis may not work with people who have deep-rooted or serious shortcomings. This may be as a result of grave psychological aberrations, distorted personal perceptions, etc. resulting in advanced attitude and behaviour problems. In other instances, a personnel problem may be magnified and made into an explosive issue. In such situations, you can take the following steps:

1. Discuss the problem person or situation with the concerned people in the organization. It is a good idea to discuss serious difficulties with regard to some people, as soon as necessary, with your personnel and industrial relations man, or his equivalent in your situation, in addition to discussing it with your boss/superior. By the very nature of their position in the organisation, they will serve as helpful experts to assist you in handling the situation. A word of caution: Do not wait till the situation becomes virtually

hopeless before discussing it with the personnel department and your boss. Caution them as soon as you feel that a serious problem may result. This will get you their support and help if the situation does deteriorate and result in a grave problem.

The new purchase manager of a light engineering factory discovered that orders for fork lift trucks were being manipulated by one of his maintenance foremen. This foreman had been with the company for a long time and had a good relationship with all the key people. He did small personal favors for the senior managers whenever he could in order to stay in their good books. When sending in requests for fork lift trucks and parts, he used his influence to recommend what he wanted. Since the earlier purchasing manager did not understand or question technical requirements, the foreman had managed to get orders placed through middlemen at about twice the normal costs of equivalent brands. Obviously, the foreman was pocketing most of the illicit earnings.

Since ordering of maintenance equipment was done on a continuous basis, the new purchasing manager found that dealing with the foreman was becoming a problem. The foreman was very courteous and pleasant, but always dictated what he wanted. He even got approvals from the maintenance manager and the general manager whenever necessary. The new purchasing manager wanted to do things efficiently and economically. It was while reviewing the past files that he discovered that the well-known foreman had cost the company thousands of rupees extra every month in the past and was still continuing to do so. Before it became more serious he decided to discuss the matter with the personnel and the general manager. He also mentioned it confidentially to the President of the company. The general manager knew the foreman for a long time and could hardly believe what he was told. In fact, he implied that as the purchasing manager was new in the position, maybe he didn't fully understand the technical needs of the maintenance department. The general manager, nevertheless, promised to warn the maintenance foreman and discuss the matter with him. The maintenance foreman, in the meantime, had learned about what the new purchasing manager was attempting to do. He countered with whatever emotional and technical support he could gather to prove that he was above reproach. The relevant papers from the maintenance file in the purchase department mysteriously disappeared. The foreman saw to it that through some of his friends, allegations were made against the new purchasing manager, saying that he accepted lavish invitation and gifts from interested suppliers. The President appointed a committee consisting of the Vice President of Operations, the Head Office General Manager and the factory's Personnel and Administration manager to investigate the case. Because the new purchasing manager had discussed the problem situation with the relevant people in the organization before it deteriorated into a fight for survival, his report carried organization before it deteriorated into a fight for survival, his report carried significant weight. Had he waited and reported the corruption activity after allegations against him had been made, the report would have been viewed differently. The committee of internal experts which investigated the situation recommended the discharge of the problem foreman and commended the efforts of the new purchasing manager in handling the situation with foresight.

With experience, it has been learnt that successful managers refer and discuss potentially serious difficulties with internal experts in the organization as early as possible. They avoid waiting till the last moment, when help may or may not be forthcoming.

2. Ask for the help of the relevant outside experts whenever necessary. Some problem employees or situations cannot be effectively tackled with internal resources alone. Whenever desirable, helpful outside experts should be involved to resolve the difficult situation. Thus, depending upon the situation, psychologists, legal experts, renowned mediators and arbitrators, management consultants or others, can be referred to the problem. Problem people with attitude constraints should be selectively sponsored for outside sensitivity training sessions and relevant management courses given by experts, when there is a reasonable chance that they will benefit from these exposures.

Sometimes a situation involves a problem group. In that case, experts on group dynamics may be called in to organize beneficial group sessions to reduce stress within an organization and to realign group objectives. In some situations legal advice, at the right time, can help thwart a bad situation from developing further. Outside mediators and arbitrators are often a great help, particularly when they are called in as soon as it is apparent that outside assistance would be beneficial.

A factory was involved in a labor dispute with its local union. The industrial relations manager and general manager had had several meetings with the union representative, but to no avail. A mutual distrust between the two parties developed. Each doubted the intentions of the other of really implementing what the other had said. The industrial relations manager realized that outside mediation, by a mutually acceptable labor expert, would help in bringing about an early settlement. There was a labor expert available who had himself been a union leader at one time, and was now a well respected and renowned politician. The local union would certainly approve of him. The industrial relations manager knew that the labor expert could be depended upon for an equitable solution. He discussed the matter with him. The labor expert was very helpful and agreed to mediate. Since both parties trusted him, it was not long before an acceptable solution was reached to end the labor unrest.

Not all managers, however, utilize outside resources as well as the industrial relations manager did in the above example. Some managers do not even explore the possibility of getting outside experts to help. This is a mistake. Referring serious difficulties to outside experts is sometimes the only way a difficult personnel problem can be solved without much damage and expense.

Adapting Problem People to Group Objectives

One noticeable behaviour most problem people exhibit, is that they tend to do things individually, disregarding group objectives. It could be because of egoism, mental slowness, laziness or ineptitude. They tend to be non-cooperative. They only way to make them adapt to group objectives is to appeal to their unfulfilled needs (such as self-esteem, affiliation or recognition). This can motivate them to produce cooperative group behaviour.

It can be done in a practical manner by taking the following steps:

1.   Give the responsibility for meeting group objectives due importance. It is certainly motivating to have one's responsibility recognized explicitly as being important to the group. By conveying to the problem person, in a suitable manner, that his work is important for the achievement of group objectives, you will be motivating him towards accomplishing the work. However, for this to work, the subsequent steps must also be followed.

2.   Establish group goals and rewards that can be shared. To motivate cooperative behaviour, it is beneficial to provide goals and rewards that can also be shared individually by the group members.

3.   Let them feel they are wanted. The worst thing to do is to treat a problem person as a villain. If you are working to adapt him to group tasks, make sure you give him the feeling that he is wanted because of the work he is capable of doing. Experience has shown that most problem people are victims of circumstances and want to gain acceptance if given an honorable opportunity to do so.

4.   Provide opportunities for team assignments in which problem people are interested. Assign problem people to areas of their interest. Let them join the committees or group assignments they would like to work on. This must

be done in a casual manner, as most problem people do not like to be treated special since that would make them conscious of their shortcomings. By arranging to see that they work on committees or assignments which match their interest, you will motivate in them a desire for teamwork so that they achieve the things they want to. This is known to help in improving their behaviour in other areas of work as well.

5. Utilize Sensitivity training sessions to generate an appreciation for effective group dynamics. If a problem employee is psychologically stable, his participation in a sensitivity training program will help to adapt him to work better in a group environment. He will become more deeply aware of the impact of interpersonal relationships and cooperative behaviour on group performance. Such programs are likely to make him more sensitive to group needs and adapt his behaviour accordingly.

By following the above steps in the order most pertinent to your own situation, you will be able to provide strong motivation to your problem people enabling them to adapt their behaviour towards group objectives.

Changing Problem People into Assets
There are four recognized ways by which you can change a problem person into an asset. These are:
1. By restructuring his assignment so as to give him the work he can handle satisfactorily.
2. By relocating him to an assignment he can cope with competently.
3. By rehabilitating him in his present assignment through promoting his individual development and providing supervisory guidance.
4. By replacing him with a person better suited to do the job.

Ofcourse, the option selected depends upon the situation and the problem employee concerned. To be able to correctly decide upon the right step to be taken, it is necessary to isolate the negative factors responsible for the problem employee's performance and behaviour. There are twelve such factors which are readily recognizable and have a significant influence in causing undesirable behaviour. An understanding of the following 12 factors is certainly important in order to isolate and resolve them.

1. **Job Knowledge:** To perform well, an individual must have the necessary knowledge and skills at his disposal. When individuals are placed on assignments for which they are not properly prepared, performance will suffer until the needed know-how is acquired.

2. **Family relationships:** Individuals who have family disputes spend so much time thinking and sorting them out that their performance is affected adversely. When family worries are carried to the job and necessary attention cannot be given to work assignments, a significant drop in performance level is discernable.

3. **Social Values:** Some jobs require a highly developed sense of fair play, other assignments that conflict with individual values create blocks and thereby deter good performance.

4. **Supervisory support:** Poor supervision of individuals leads to poor performance. When support is withheld and directions change frequently, it results in poor levels of performance. When supervisors do not organize and plan properly, employee effectiveness is harmed.

5. **Physical fitness:** Employees must measure up to jobs physically. Significant health shortcomings may prevent employees from doing demanding jobs effectively.

6. **Living and working environment:** Some individuals are more sensitive, than others, to their surroundings. Climate, size of the community or even recreational facilities lead to problems in particular cases. Poor facilities, inadequate tools, and other substandard aspects of an employee's working environment also cause frustrated and undesirable reactions. Problem employees are often unwilling victims of their surroundings.

7. **Organizational policies:** In some situations, organizational policies may be too restrictive. Employees need a certain measure of operating freedom in order to perform effectively. Policies that disregard this need can result in dysfunctional behaviour.

8. **Inadequate intelligence:** Employees must have the capacity to acquire the necessary knowledge and skills, as well as, learn new things to improve their performance. When this is lacking, opportunities to develop are not of much help.

9. **Emotional strengths:** An employee whose emotional make-up is not in harmony with the demands of his work, he cannot perform satisfactorily. Before he can be effective, this mismatch must be removed.

10. **Group interaction:** When some individuals cannot get along with each other, the output of each person falls. Bickering, petty jealousies, rudeness and arrogance keeps individual and group performance low.

11. **Inadaptability:** An employee who cannot cope with new changes in functional requirements often exhibits problematic behaviour.

12. **Organizational identification:** An individual who doesn't support the objectives, goals, procedures and practices of the organization he works for cannot get fully committed to its operations. This affects his performance adversely.

These negative factors, which generate dysfunctional behaviour in employees, must be isolated and surmounted before employees deemed 'problematic' can be changed into assets. In each problem employee, one or more of these factors are operable. How can one surmount or resolve these negative factors is illustrated by the following case examples.

Case 1 (Restructuring Assignments)

Vinod had been promoted to the position of National Sales and Services Director of a large corporation. He found that his subordinate, Vinay, in-charge of sales and service for one of the product groups, was constantly having service problems. Vinay did a good job of organizing sales but neglected service functions. This was becoming a serious handicap. Vinod gave the matter careful consideration and decided to utilize Vinay's sales strengths by restructuring the product groupings into sales and services as separate functions and placing Vinay in-charge of Sales. Another manager, Raj Kumar, who had been responsible for sales and service for the other product group, was proficient in service rather than in sales and was therefore given the responsibility for service functions in the restructured organization. Vinay and Raj Kumar, both of whom had been problem individuals in different areas, began to turn in good performances in their restructured assignments.

Case 2 (Relocating Individuals)

Brijesh was a Sales Manager whose performance was adversely affected by his asthmatic condition. He had the ability but lacked the high energy levels essential for good performance. Realizing this, the Vice President in charge of sales transferred him from New Delhi to the company's branch sales office at Cochin. There, Brijesh's asthma disappeared and he became one of the company's top producers.

Case 3 (Rehabilitating Employees)

Jaideep was brought in from a competitive organization to head the administration department of a large sales organization. He found that he had a problem employee in Trisha who was the supervisor in charge of equipment order entry and control. Trisha made many mistakes and her day to day working was becoming quite a problem. Jaideep was thinking of letting Trisha go and hiring a substitute. He checked to see how Trisha had done in her previous assignment. He was a little surprised to find that it was Trisha's earlier excellent performance in sales that had earned her a promotion into the administrative department. Trisha had been interested in an administration assignment. It was obvious however, that Trisha did not have any previous experience in an administrative job. Jaideep suggested that one of his top assistants work closely with Trisha to give her continuous counsel and guidance till she became more proficient in her new responsibilities. Trisha was also sponsored for some seminars that would help her develop necessary administrative skills. This approach to rehabilitate Trisha paid-off. Primarily, because she had the capacity to acquire additional skills and knowledge. Within a few months, Trisha became an asset rather than a liability for the administration department.

Case 4 (Replacing Individuals)

Mohit managed the accounts department of a reputed organization. He had a problem employee who wanted to do things his own way. Mohit knew that the employee was not an organization man. His analysis had shown that the problem could not be solved by restructuring him. The employee was interested in the arts and painting. Mohit advised him to use his time more fruitfully in trying to do what he could do well, that is, paint portraits. He took Mohit's advice, and set up a small stall in the major shopping center of the town to make pencil portraits of interested shoppers. Before this employee left, Mohit asked for the necessary approval and hired a person who could handle the job with greater interest and proficiency. This change proved extremely beneficial, as the department replaced a problem worker with one who did the work well.

These examples illustrate how you can change problem people into assets. Your choice of the method would depend upon the situation and the individual's negative factors contributing to the problem. The four approaches discussed here can yield a high return with respect to the time you allocate to change problem people into assets. Your success in managing such people will depend upon how well you follow such an approach.

Having covered the various behaviorial aspects of interacting with people, now is the time to learn the practical approach to Effective Persuasion Skills (EPS) discussed in the next chapter.

Chapter 6

THE PRACTICAL APPROACH TO
EFFECTIVE PERSUASION SKILLS (EPS)
A Predictive & Proven Scientific System of
Persuasion which you can Control

Is persuasion an art?

Can persuasion skills be learnt?

As established earlier on, Effective Persuasion Skills depend upon proper understanding of the human behaviour. Human behaviour is predictable and lends itself to scientific analysis. Therefore, persuasion skills can be learnt.

It is for this reason that behavioural science has emerged as being very important and is being taught in practically every important management institution all over the world. Because it is a science, it clearly implies that just like one can learn physics and chemistry one can also learn human behaviour.

Effective persuasion skills therefore comprise of a predictive and proven scientific system of persuasion that one can control after understanding and internalising it. The only qualification required to learn effective persuasion skills is a real desire to do so. It is a simple yet a very powerful body of knowledge that can help bring great achievements, happiness and understanding in one's day-to-day performance. These skills can help improve individual performance in both personal and occupational capacities; whether one is a student, house-wife, teacher, executive, senior manager, chairman, scientist, politician, salesman, farmer or whoever.

The Effective Persuasion Skills (EPS) model covers the following steps / phases / skill progressions:

1. **Opening Statement (O)**

   During a heated Presidential debate with Hillary Clinton, Barack Obama opened his statements with, "I agree with what Hillary has said..." before he went onto present his point of view.

   Opening statements are crucial. They introduce the broad benefit or idea that can help satisfy the other person's interests or needs. They also help to set the right tone or intention.

2. **Probing (P)**

   Correct probing skills help you do the following:
   i)   Evaluate the other person's attitude & needs
   ii)   Set up supporting statements
   iii) Proceed in a non-direct manner, especially when you want to discuss things the other person feels are important
   iv)   Proceed in a direct manner when you want to discuss things which you feel are important
   v)   Proceed to the next step when your initial attempt to get a commitment or acceptance has not been successful.

3. **Objection Handling (O)**

   The attitude of the person being pursued can be categorised into:
   a) Acceptance   b) Indifference   c) Objection
   Objections can be categorised as : i) Easy or ii) Difficult
   Just like the antidote to a chemical reaction can be scientifically analyzed and implemented, similarly objections can be handled in a predictable and scientific manner through a disciplined approach.

   a) In case of : **Acceptance**
   Additional benefits should be introduced and a close made to get the commitment of the person.

   b) In case of: **Indifference**
   Probing should be done in a direct manner to uncover dissatisfactions, needs and expectations which can then be tackled as per the guidelines provided.

   c) In case of : **Objection**
   For all objections, both easy or difficult, you must reinstate the objection in question form. This makes sure that the objection is properly understood. Since in majority of cases, actual objections are perceived very differently and this makes acceptance or commitment, at worst, practically impossible and

at best, delayed.

i) Easy objections should be answered directly, offering proof as answer.

ii) Difficult objections should be handled by stressing on other relevant benefits of the proposition, so as to minimise the genuine disadvantages, if any.

4. **Proving statements (P)**

Proving statements are used to remove doubts that the other person may have about your idea or proposition. While making proving statements, a strict discipline must be followed. That is:

i) Restating the benefits of your proposal or idea

ii) Proving it.

iii) Expanding it.

5. **Supporting statement (S)**

Supporting statements make use of and build on favourable remarks made by the other person. There are two ways to go about it. You may offer agreement or reinforcement to the other person's favourable remark. Or you may want to introduce an appropriate benefit relevant to the person.

6. **Closing skills (C)**

Closing is getting acceptance or commitment to what you want. There are many closing techniques that are used and we will discuss these powerful practical techniques in detail further on.

EPS (Effective Persuasion Skills) can be acquired by following a particular discipline and the right attitude. The acronym is: OPOS-PC. Right from the first O to the C, you will be able to close an argument or get a ready "Yes" to your idea or proposal when you imbibe the following attitudinal/behavioural/psychological aspects:

a) You must assume that the acceptance/commitment from the other person already exists

b) You must summarise important benefits to the other person for accepting your proposal / idea.

c) You must ask for explicit acceptance of your proposal / idea.

The EPS model with its six behavioural phases is aimed at getting acceptance. The most successful people who are capable and have the power of conviction and the ability to get acceptance advertently or inadvertently follow these behavioural patterns.

The most important aspect around which the EPS model centers is, CLOSING. Some top individual performers worldwide start with a CLOSE itself aimed at getting acceptance in the shortest possible time. In case the acceptance does not come in the first attempt, then other phases of handling objections, probing etc. are done till another CLOSING attempt is made. This is repeated till a proper understanding is reached and acceptance obtained.

In the following chapters, we will use practical examples to look in detail, at each phase of the EPS model. We will learn how to develop the skills required for handling each phase to get the desired results.

CHAPTER 7

THE OPENING STATEMENT (O)
How Should you open a Conversation?

How many times have you felt a little jittery or uncertain in starting conversations about something you wanted? Usually, one is a little hesitant to ask for acceptance or commitment because of the fear of rejections directly or indirectly. The skills outlined below, especially the Initial Benefit Statement (IBS) will help you to overcome the difficulty of opening conversations and getting a Yes from the other person on your idea or proposal. Once you are clear about what you need acceptance on and also learn how to satisfy and make the other person happy / positive, you will become more dynamic and effective in not only opening the conversation but also in achieving the objectives.

Since this is a very crucial step /phase in the EPS model, strict rules are to be followed and the reader is advised that these be treated as scientifically tried and tested rules to be followed without exception.

The Initial Benefit Statement (IBS) must always begin with a general benefit and then refer specifically to the idea/product. The reason for starting with a general benefit is to attract the attention of the other person since everyone is interested in general benefit. To give an everyday example, if you are wanting to get the other person/persons interest in going out on a picnic, instead of suggesting "let's go out on a picnic to leisure valley", it is much more effective to open the conversation by stating that "outings help in relaxing the mind and getting some fresh air is extremely good for the mind and body." With this kind of general benefit, your specific proposal will be accepted much better by everyone. Another example -
A Salesman trying to persuade his customer to buy a copier – It would be advisable for him to open the conversation with the general benefits of having a

copier machine rather than talking specifically about his product. The sales pitch would be more effective if he were to say, for instance," Office productivity increase is an important aspect for all progressive organizations. One method to increase office productivity is to have an in-house copying facility."

After making such an Initial Benefit Statement you can proceed along and talk about your idea / product in specific details. For better understanding, let me highlight the uses of **Initial Benefit Statement (IBS).**

IBS is designed to:
1. Get the interest of the other person / customer
2. Get a positive reaction
3. Justify your taking up the time
4. Use the background information you have
5. Give reasons for the discussion
6. Introduce yourself or your idea / product in a way that is logical from the other's point of view

It can also be used to:
7. Obtain agreement on the objective for the meeting
8. Initiate the understanding of the needs of the other person
9. Summarize the benefits of your idea / product offers
10. Introduce other benefits later in a discussion
11. Introduce new ideas / products
12. Summarize past calls / discussions

IBS may be used:
13. At the beginning of a sales call or the start of a conversation
14. When the other person / customer indicates that you should get down to business / the real purpose of your visit.
15. When you wish to introduce a completely different topic (benefit, idea or proposal)
16. When you wish to change your communication objective, to explain 'the why' to the other person/customer during a meeting.

In relation to other EPS skills, it can be used:
17. To introduce a series of probes to clarify the other person's / customer's reaction to your statement.
18. To prepare for a series of support statements.

After the opening benefit statement it is important to probe for understanding the other person better.

Chapter 8

PROBING (P)
How to Understand the other Person's needs Better

Probing is a scientific method of initiating questions. The response to these questions can help you understand the needs of the other person.
It is important that you probe when you want:

1) To evaluate the other person's needs, attitudes, etc.
   This is best done by asking questions such as what does the other person think about the situation or what are the needs/expectations of the other person from a product, system, service, idea, etc.

2) To set up supporting statements
   Probing is an opportunity to provide supporting statements in response to a favourable remark made by the other person. They help create a more congenial atmosphere.

3) To gain acceptance for some of your beneficial and factual statements
   Probing should be done in an indirect manner especially when you want to discuss things which are important to the other person. As an example, one can ask, "what features, according to you, are extremely important in a system?" or "what do you feel are the advantages you will get by purchasing this system" or "what are you looking from a holiday during your summer vacation?" These probing statements are presented in an indirect manner and the response will bring out points / views which are important to the other person.

4) When acceptance of the idea does not seem likely to take place immediately.
   Probing should be done in a direct manner when you want to discuss things which you feel are important. An example, "don't you think having a copying machine can help improve the office productivity and also further organizational performance?", or "don't you think

for a hill station is ideal for a summer vacation? Especially one where you can relax and rejuvenate and also enjoy the company of good friends?".

Probing is a powerful skill to effectively determine the actual state of mind of the other person so that you are better informed and develop a greater understanding. This understanding will determine whether you get a Yes or not.

5) The probing statement may also be used to determine the reservations or hesitations of the other person, if any.

Let me objectively summarize for better understanding. Let us say X is the person being probed or X is the customer.

Indirect Probing is to obtain information on:
1. The past situation of X.
2. The present situation of X.
3. Problems that X knows about or is willing to admit.
4. Why a close was not successful in the first place.
5. When X is still uncertain and is not accepting any proof.
6. Competitive products that X is presently using.
7. X's Attitudes and interests.
8. Friends or sources of information that X respects.
9. Reasons for X's hesitancy, reluctance, doubt or unwillingness to go ahead.
10. Objections that are hidden.
11. Criteria used for making decisions.
12. Biases or prejudices (not usually spelled out).
13. The importance that X places on something related to your proposition.
14. Draw out or encourage X.
15. Indicate that you have further interest in an area
16. Make your discussion relevant to X's needs.
17. Give X an opportunity to express his / her opinions / feelings.

Direct Probing is to obtain confirmation as to:
1. How important a benefit is to X.
2. Whether he / she has accepted your proof statement.
3. Whether you have understood clearly what was said by X.
4. What priority or how much importance X places on a need or a particular problem.
5. Whether X has accepted a claim you have made about your product.
6. Whether X has in fact accepted your closing statement.
7. X's attitude towards a point that is being discussed.
8. The significance of an objection that X has raised.

9. Whether the objection raised is the only objection or there are more.
10. Whether X largely agrees or disagrees with you.

It can also be used to:
11. Uncover problems, needs, or dissatisfactions that X was unaware of or unwilling to talk about initially.
12. Confirm periodically that you are on target in understanding what is important to X.
13. Eliminate alternatives in verifying a particular point.
14. Control the direction where you wish the discussion to move-in your favour.

Direct Probing can be used anytime. Often it is used soon after indirect probes have not brought out the information you want. In relation to other EPS skills, it can be used to lead the other person / customer to make statements that you can support.

Probing will often lead to Objections and the next phase of the EPS Model is Objection Handling.

Chapter 9

OBJECTION HANDLING (O)
How to Change Objections to Acceptance?

How many times have you felt stumped by objections from the other person to which you do not have a convincing response? It is interesting to know that objections can be scientifically analysed and handled. You can develop skills to convert them into acceptance situations rather than frustrating no-nos.

For this, it is important to understand the nature of objections as well as the attitude of the person being pursued. It can be:

a) **Acceptance.**
    When the other person appears favourably inclined to your point of view. In this case, you should share additional benefits and ask for commitments.

b) **Indifference.**
    When the other person is nonchalant or indifferent to your idea. In this case, you need to probe in a direct manner to uncover areas of dissatisfaction. As an example, you may ask, "What is it that you do not like about the idea?".

c) **Objections.**
    These can be:
    i)   **Easy Objections:** where you feel confident that you can handle the doubt, answer in a direct manner, offering proofs, if necessary.
    ii) **Difficult Objections:** when the other person has valid unfavourable points about your ideas or proposals, one can best handle the situation by stressing other relevant benefits that are more significant than the objections raised.

There is one Golden rule which is proved to be priceless while handling objections. The Golden rule is:

Whenever you hear an objection, without exception, you must re-state the same in question form before answering.

This Golden rule is based on the fact that communication is often subject to mis-understandings. Often in an inter-personal dialogue between two or more people, it is quite possible that only one person really understands what is spoken and the others just don't get it. This also has to do with the complexity of human nature. Often when we are speaking to someone, his brain is working simultaneously. At the same time, we are anticipating a response as soon as he starts talking. Very often this results in misunderstanding and not getting what the other person is really trying to communicate. In order to be sure that you have fully understood the other person's point, it is necessary for you to repeat the objection in question form. Let us take a simple example.

> *If Mr. X tells you that he has reservations about your idea because of the costs involved, it is necessary for you to re-phrase the objection in question form as follows: "If I understand you correctly, you have reluctance to accept the idea because of the costs involved?" The other person can sometimes reply to clarify the objections by saying "No, I am not concerned about the initial cost but I am more concerned about the recurring costs of the system. If the recurring cost is low, I don't mind paying a higher cost for the system." If you had not re-phrased the objection in question form you may have proceeded to answer the objection without realizing that he is open to paying a higher cost if the recurring cost is low.*

Very few people discipline themselves to re-phrase objections in question form before answering them. You start following this Golden rule and you will be amazed at how you start understanding the real objections more quickly and get quicker acceptance than you would have got in the past.

This requires discipline and restraint because as an impulse, our first reaction to an objection is to reply to it immediately based on our understanding of it in the first instance. Since what you may have understood in the first instance can be erroneous, re-phrasing the objections in question form, is a simple, logical and powerful way of getting better understanding and a quicker "Yes" to your idea.

Objections and The Salesperson

Selling isn't always smooth sailing and if you see enough prospects, you are bound to run into your share of objections. But minus objections, sales people would be reduced to nothing more than glorified order-takers and commission rates would be a fraction of their present size and selling would no longer be a prosperous career. So be grateful for the objections. After all, you don't see anyone getting rich selling tickets in those tiny booths in front of movie theatres.

Ofcourse this does not mean that I enjoy being bombarded with objections. I don't look forward to them any more than you do. But years ago I realized that I had to deal with objections to succeed in sales and ever since, I have confronted them vigorously. I accept them as part of the business. In fact, in my complete career as a salesperson, I'd estimate that 80 percent of the sales I closed were the ones where I encountered at least one objection. As you can see, if I had stopped selling every time someone didn't want to buy from me, I would have been knocked out of the business years ago.

One way to reduce the number of objections your encounter is to give a thorough sales presentation. The more complete the sales pitch, the more clearly the buyer will understand your offer, which in turn will provide him with more reasons to make a positive buying decision. There have been times when I tried to give a watered down presentation because I was trying to make a quick sale in time for my next appointment, or I was simply tired from being overworked. Whatever the reason, whenever I did that, I ended up having to answer a series of objections and as a result, found myself spending more time than I would have, if I had given a full presentation in the first place.

Another way to reduce objections is by realizing that some objections are raised with enough regularity to become predictable. A seasoned salesperson will incorporate the answers to some common objections into the sales presentation. So you can address the objections before they are raised. Or you can keep effective answers in reserve, to draw upon when seldom-raised objections do crop up again.

You must realize that your answer to every objection doesn't have to be 100% satisfactory. It is not mandatory to have the perfect product for every customer. Just imagine if you had insisted on perfection when you selected your spouse, or if your spouse had sought perfection when choosing you, there would be much amiss. You both had to settle for a few shortcomings because the other qualities were especially appealing. You can apply this thinking to every aspect of your life. There is no such thing as a perfect career, house, investment and so on. Nothing is perfect. Life is full of compromises. If people made choices only for perfection, nothing would ever be decided.

With this in mind, if your prospect doesn't like every feature of your product, don't assume you have lost the sale. After all, your competition won't have a perfect product either. When I sold projects, I didn't always have a project that was better, feature by feature, than all others. All I needed were enough good features to convince people to buy what I had to sell.

Objections are Expressions of Interest
When I tell salespeople that prospects are expressing interest when they raise objections, I sometimes get looks that suggest I have gone off the deep end. "There has got to be a better way for prospects to express themselves", one salesman told me.

It would be wonderful if all prospects would sign their names on the dotted lines and whip out their cheque books at the appropriate time in your sales presentation. But as you and I both know, it is just not that easy. Instead, people can be subtle about letting you know their interest. And sometimes those subtleties go right over your head. Often people will raise objections to gather more reasons not to buy. And at these points, rather than hanging in there, many salespeople will give up and go on to the next call.

I have always believed that when somebody tells me why he doesn't want to buy my product, he is expressing a willingness to listen to why he should buy. As a matter of fact, I welcome objections in this context because I like people who become seriously involved. It is the individual who listens to a sales presentation and says nothing who's a far more difficult person to sell. He only shakes his head and makes negative comments such as "I'm not interested", I don't like it" and "I don't want to buy". These are the most difficult because he isn't objecting to anything specific. It is as if the sales presentation had no effect on him whatsoever. Neither does he care to challenge the value of the product in question nor your statement on product quality nor asks for proof that will solve his problem. People who care about your product, but aren't convinced enough to buy, will vent their objections. I interpret these objections as positive signs. I know that if I properly handle their questions, I will make the sale. For example, a prospect has a computer system, and replacing it with your model will cost him more money. When he says that perhaps he should continue with his present system to save money; he's asking for assurance that he will benefit from buying your model. But if he only says, "I will stay with my present model", there is little for you to sink your teeth into. Unless you do some probing to uncover his actual objections, the chances of your making a sale are nil.

Some examples of objections with hidden requests for additional information are:

Objection: *I don't think this represents the best value for my rupee.*
Hidden Request: *I challenge you to prove that your product provides an excellent value for my money.*

Objection: *This size doesn't appear to be best for me.*
Hidden Request: *Prove to me that this is my correct size.*

Question: *I have never heard of your company.*
Hidden request: *I want to buy from you, I need to know that your company is a trustworthy and reliable firm.*

Objection: *I am trying to reduce expenses, so I'm not in the mind for anything new.*
Hidden request: *Unless you can convince me that your product is really something that I need, I won't buy.*

Objection: *I'm going to shop around and see what else is available.*
Hidden request: *You haven't sold me anything. Either keep selling so I'll be convinced to buy now or I'm taking a walk.*

Ideally, the prospect will explain why he prefers his present system over yours. For instance, he might say, "My present model has the capacity to process my accounts receivables daily and yours doesn't." Or he might tell you, "XYZ machines have a wonderful service contract, and whenever there's a problem, they attend within twenty -four hours." With this information, you can zero in on the prospect's objection. Now it's a matter of convincing the prospect of what you can provide. Your computer has more capacity than his present one, and as a result it will save him time, provide more information, better serve his customers and reduce downtime because your company's average service call is performed within three and a half hours of the request.

When a prospect is getting outstanding service from an existing source, it's naturally more difficult to win the account. Understandably, people are loyal to those uncommonly rare salespeople and companies that take good care of their customers. For instance, a prospect says to a stockbroker, "I'm quite satisfied with my present broker. I've made money with her and she gives me excellent service. Besides, she's a good friend."

Even this statement doesn't mean there is no chance of winning this prospect over. Here's a good response is "I am happy to know that you are in such good hands. It's nice to hear such things. But I am sure that you will agree that no stockbroker has a monopoly on fine ideas, so with your permission I'd like to keep in touch with you. At some time in the future when what I consider an unusual opportunity to take a position in a particular company, I will give you a call. Certainly you have no objection to my doing this, do you?

Real Objections Versus False Objections

For a variety of reasons, people will give false objections rather than telling you why they really don't want to buy. Obviously, unless you know the real objections, you probably won't be able to overcome what's truly bothering your prospect. Bombarding him with facts that have nothing to do with the real objections won't change his mind. For instance:

Aman, a stockbroker, is attempting to secure an order for 5000 shares of ATR Corporation. Client, Sameer who happens to be his neighbour and a close friend, voices the objection that he invests in growth companies.

"ATR had a loss of two rupees a share for the year", Sameer objects.

"Yes, but the company had a non-recurring write-off, and our analysts estimate that next year earnings will come in at ten rupees a share." Says Aman.

"I'll believe it when I see it. The company hasn't made any money for nine quarters," Sameer says.

In reality, Sameer's actual objection is that his nephew is now selling securities, and he plans to use him as his broker (he's under strict orders from is wife). However, he doesn't want to hurt Aman's feelings, as he has been his stockbroker for twenty years. Sameer simply doesn't know how to gracefully explain to his old friend that he won't be doing business with him in the future and using his nephew instead. No matter how hard Aman attempts to sell Sameer, (on the estimated annual earnings of ATR), he will not persuade him to make the investment because those facts have nothing to do with the real objection. Unless, Aman realizes that the nephew is the real reason for Sameer not buying and deals with it directly, Sameer is not going to give the order to execute a transaction in his name.

There are dozens of reasons prospects express, and unless you are able to weed out the real objections, you will miss out on a lot of sales. It is also quite probable that a prospect might not know enough about your company but doesn't want to offend you by suggesting that it may be an unreliable or dishonest firm. Instead, he says: "I'd like to sleep on it." In this situation, you might give him several excellent reasons why it is urgent to act now, such as a shortage of inventory, an expected price increase, or a significant loss he will suffer by putting off the purchase. None of these facts, however, will convince him that you represent a legitimate, trustworthy company.

One of the common objections people don't like to express is that they can't afford to buy your product. It's embarrassing to admit they don't have enough money. It hurts their pride. So rather than saying they can't afford it, people offer false excuses ranging from "I have a brother-in-law in the business" to "I want to wait until the new models are available." And so on. As you can surmise, unless one is able to size up these prospects correctly, one can talk until he was blue in the face and never overcome their real objections. Once you know the real reason, you could talk about trade-in allowances, monthly payments, and a variety of other solutions to convince them that they could, after all afford to buy a car.

Perhaps the best way to recognize false objections is by observing people's reaction after you provide them with solid answers. Generally, their lack of response to intelligent answers is a good clue that they're not telling you their real objection. Take, for instance, the case about Sameer's telling his stockbroker, Aman, that he had no interest in ATR Corporation because he liked growth companies for investments. After several minutes of presenting solid facts supporting his contention that ATR was, indeed, a growth company, Aman should conclude that something else was his client's real objection. After all, he knew Sameer was an otherwise reasonable and astute investor and was ignoring the strong selling points that would normally influence his buying decision.

Another clue is that when people throw a series of unrelated objections at you, it's a signal that they're covering up what really is troubling them. Eventually, you must think to yourself: Nobody can have so many real objections for not buying! Once you know this, you can begin to ask questions that will reveal the real objection.

If you still can't uncover it, you may want to bluntly ask: "Mr. Prospect, I'd like you to do me a favour." Most people are thrown back by this and will generally reply: "Sure, what is it?"
"I know that this car is perfect for you and it represents an excellent value, but I have a feeling deep inside me that there's something you haven't told me. I'd like to know the real reason you're hesitant to make a buying decision today."

"Oh, I just want to sleep on it overnight, Jai."

"Come on, what is it?"

"It's really nothing."

"Look, you can tell me. What's really the reason you don't feel comfortable buying a car tonight?"

"Well, to tell you the truth, Jai..." - and they come right out with it.

With this information, I can come back with, "I had a feeling it was something like that and I want you to know how much I appreciate you being so up-front with me." Now an otherwise lost sale has become a problem sale.

As you can see, you sometimes have to do some prodding before a prospect will tell you what's really on his mind. But you have to find out, and unless you have some fairly good ideas, I don't recommend attempting to guess because you can cover the entire waterfront before you stumble on the real objection. In the meantime, you're liable to voice a few objections that he hadn't thought about - and in the process open a can of worms.

There are some people who swear up and down that they're not going to be pressured into buying anything - no matter what! And they're determined right from the start that they won't buy under any circumstances. For instance, a man might tell his co-workers, "A life insurance agent is stopping by tonight, but he's wasting his time as under no circumstances I am buying anything." A couple might accept a free vacation from a recreational land developer with the understanding that they will spend three hours of their weekend listening to a sales presentation. They too tell their friends, "We're just going to listen so we can enjoy a weekend out of town. We have absolutely no interest in buying one of their units." Likewise, another person tells his friends that he's going to stop in on his way home from work to look at the new models, "but no way do I intend to buy a car."

Often these people fool themselves because they end up wanting to buy but are embarrassed to face the ridicule and flak from those who tell them that they shouldn't buy. It's important to understand this behaviour in order to close the sale, and fortunately there are some clues. One is an unusual number of unrelated objections. Another could be comments such as "I'm really surprised that it's this good", and ,"So-and-so told me this was a high-pressure outfit, but you're really not, are you?" When you hear remarks such as these, you must give the prospect some extra assurance that he is making a wise decision.

Never Back a Prospect into a Corner

An important rule to remember is that you aren't in business to win the battle and lose the war. I've seen salespeople get into arguments with customers, but no matter who wins, the sale is lost. Never argue with customers because you'll end up antagonizing them.

Some objections people raise aren't worth discussing. For example, when a prospect would say to me during the beginning part of my sales presentation, "I'm just shopping around and don't intend to buy a car today," I would ignore the remark. While I thought that he probably was sincere, I knew he'd feel differently after he'd seen what I had to offer. However, most salespeople have tendency to fire back: "Why do you want to shop around? Everything you could possibly want is right here in my inventory."

Comments of this nature put the prospect on the defensive. He's backed into a corner and feels he must defend his comment. "Well, I never buy a car without comparing prices," he insists in self-defence. Then, throughout the rest of the sales presentation, the prospect feels as though he must save face and not change his mind. It now becomes a matter of honour because giving in would be a sign of weakness.

What could have been a passing comment becomes a matter of principle that has been blown out of proportion. When you put your prospects in this position, you are putting yourself in hot water.

A life insurance agent just beginning his career, recently told me about a potentially difficult prospect. I knew this young man had the makings of a great salesman by the way he handled the situation. The agent had walked across a wheat field to see a farmer who was operating a tractor. The latter was furious at the disturbance. The 6' 4" farmer said angrily to the 5' 6" agent: "I swore that I'd take the next no-good, low-down insurance agent who called on me and throw him right off my property."

Without hesitating, the young agent looked the farmer straight in the eyes and said, "Mister, before you try anything like that, you better take out all the insurance you can get."

There was a brief silence, and then a big smile appeared on the farmer's face. "Young man," he said, "let's go over to the house. I want to hear what you've got to sell."

When they entered the house, the farmer put his arm over the agent's shoulder and said to his wife, "Hey honey! This little guy thinks he can take me," and he let out a big belly laugh. The agent told me it was the easiest sale he ever made.

The incident reminds me of the time I had a man say, "If you try to pressurise me into buying a car, I'm going to throw you through the big glass showroom window."

I replied, "It's really a pleasure to make your acquaintance, Sir. You know something; I can tell that this is the beginning of a wonderful friendship." And it was. Over the years, I sold him six cars. Do you see how a potentially difficult situation can be made into a favourable one. Rather than starting a fight with the prospect, I won him over with my wit and charm.

Overcoming the Six Most Common Objections

Obviously, there are real objections that cannot be ignored. You must deal with these directly to close the sale. Five basic objections are the most common in every sales field. (Please note that the "I want to think it over" objections have been omitted because they will be covered in the chapter - Overcoming Procrastination.

"I can't afford it."

This includes all objections on price, such as "It costs too much," "Your price is too high," "That's more than I want to spend," and "I can get it elsewhere for less money".

Don't overlook the possibility that perhaps your prospect really can't afford to buy your product. Some prodding may be necessary to reveal the truth. If he is telling the truth, you can offer a lower-priced alternative.

Many times when prospects express shortage of funds, they only think they can't afford it. Or you might not have provided enough reasons why your product represents an outstanding value. When a person wants a product badly enough, when he knows he will get his money's worth and when financing is available, the price objection will disappear.

One way to handle price objections is to break the cost down on a weekly, daily and even hourly basis. For instance a 4 lakh rupees car has a monthly payment of Rs. 6000 or Rs. 200 a day! When you talk about only Rs. 200 a day, the price sounds more affordable.

A copy-machine salesperson, for example, sells a Rs. 2 lakh model that costs Rs. 50000 more than the competition's. The customer has decided to buy a new copier, so the salesperson talks about the 50K difference instead of the Rs. 200000 price. He then breaks the price difference down to Rs.2000 a year over the machine's ten -year life. Based on a five-day work week, that breaks down to a price difference of less than 8 rupees a day! Next he compares the seconds per copy saved and converts this time savings into Rupees saved per year. To do this, he might ask questions such as "What does your lowest-paid entry-level employee make an hour?" After it is determined that these people are paid

Rs.30 an hour, the salesperson says: "What it boils down to is less than twelve minutes a day for the lowest-paid employee on your payroll."

Other examples:

"When you break your monthly payments down to Rs.15000 a month, Mr. Rajiv, that's less than Rs.500 a day. Are you aware that the car rental agencies get Rs.1500 a day for this model? Just think of the pleasure you'll get from driving this car. And you deserve it, don't you? If you keep the car for five years, its value will be 65 percent of what you're paying, so what we're really talking about is a cost of only Rs.50 a day!"

"This television set costs less than a glass of beer a day, and your entire family will enjoy it an average of eight hours a day every day for years!"

With some business-related products, you must show how the buyer will profit by agreeing to buy from you. Observe:

"Yes, Anu, I know this proposal will mean a substantial increase in our advertising budget, but it will generate a huge increase in sales volume, which means higher profits. In short, it will pay for itself many times over again."

"It is true that this computer system represents a major expense, Sanjay, but it will reduce your labour costs and free up four of your employees from monotonous and tedious work to move to more productive areas."

"I realize that this security system is expensive, but it will reduce your insurance cost by about rupees one thousand a month. When you take this savings into consideration you really can afford it. Isn't this true, Tarun?"

"Yes, this Rs. 5000 coat is twice as expensive than the blue one, but you love it, don't you? It's the kind of coat you'll wear for the next ten years because it's style is so elegantly basic. On the other hand you'll get tired of the blue one in a relatively short time. When you spread its cost over a ten-year period, it's a terrific value."

"These cast-iron tools cost twenty-five percent more than the others, but look at the lifetime guarantee! The Cheaper ones will break in a few years and will have to be replaced. When it comes to this kind of quality, you get far more than you pay for, Right?"

There are also some excellent reasons why it will actually cost the prospect money not to buy your product, as mentioned below:

A time-sharing salesperson selling recreational condos tells his prospect: "When the cost of your condo over the next fifteen years is spread out by dividing the price of this unit at Rs. 60 lakhs that's only Rs.4 lakhs per yearly vacation. After you take inflation into consideration, you'll be spending peanuts for your vacations over the years. I 'm not even including the appreciation of your unit. I estimate *that this package will double in value during the next five to seven years. With this in mind, your vacations won't cost you anything – it will be as if you're being paid to take them."*

Likewise, a private jet, a co-op apartment for business use in Mumbai, and even the purchase of an office building could be sold on the basis that the owner will realize long-term savings rather than spending money by making a buying decision.

"I want to talk it over with my spouse."

(Included in this category are "I want to discuss it with my partner," "I want to run it by my accountant," "I want to review it with my attorney," etc.)

Perhaps the best way to avoid this objection is to make sure all decision makers are there for the sales presentation. This is done by saying something such as: "Mr. Gupta, I will be at your office on Wednesday afternoon at three-fifteen sharp. I strongly recommend that you have whoever is necessary to make a decision present." If he replies, "I'm the decision maker," then it's appropriate to say, "It's a pleasure to meet a person who has the ability to make a decision on his own without a committee to do it for him," This sets the stage for the time of the sales presentation.

This technique also works the same way when selling to married couples. "Will it be necessary to have your wife present to share in the decision making, Mr. Mehta?" If the answer is 'yes', "You'd better have her there". If he says no, then you say, "It's a pleasure to meet a man who can make a decision on his own." If the spouse is available, you can say: "Is it necessary to have your wife join us at this meeting for a decision to be made? If so, she sure is welcome." Of course if she's not, let her sit it out.

A lawn-care salesperson told me about an effective way he sells to housewives in the exclusive suburbs of Delhi. "When a housewife says that she has to talk it over with her husband, I ask, 'How much do you spend on groceries each week, ma'am?'

"'Oh, about Rs.2500 a week,' she replies.

"Do you talk it over with your husband each time before you go to the supermarket?" I ask.

"'Yet you spend more than one lakh twenty thousand rupees a year on your groceries. That's quite a big expenditure, and one I notice doesn't require his permission. Well, we're only talking about a two thousand rupees-a-month decision, so I'm sure he won't mind your making it, will *he?' I then assume the sale by adding, 'would you like for my crew to come on Wednesday morning or afternoon?"*

When a potential car buyer told me he wanted to talk it over with his wife at the end of a sales presentation and she wasn't there, I'd say: "In the meantime, let's put the order through, Go ahead and put your okay right here, will you? And I need five thousand rupees as a deposit." The first time he'd say it, I'd ignore the remark rather making an issue out of it. If the prospect was the macho type, I'd add: "You know something, Harish, it's a real treat to deal with a man like you who's capable of making up his own mind. There are too many guys these days who let their wives call all of the shots."
If he'd still say, "No, Jagdish, I have to talk to her," I'd add, "Let's get the order processed and you can go home and tell her about it. Or better yet, bring her down here and explain the benefit to her against it, you can have your deposit back." In the vast majority of cases, these deals went through. But if the customer walked out without making a deposit, the chances were great that I'd lost the sales because he wouldn't come back. Of course, when a woman comes in without her husband, I naturally tell her how much I admire today's women who make buying decisions without their husband's permission.

"I have a good friend in the business."
(Or it could be a brother-in-law, a mother-in-law, or a next door neighbor, etc. who sells the same thing you sell.)

Here you must ask yourself: "Is the prospect interested in giving business to his friend or doing what is best for himself?" Generally, most people want to better themselves rather than making a poor purchase at their own expense.

When a stockbroker hears this objection, he replies: "Harish, I understand how you feel toward your friend. But I am sure you would agree that you need to do what is best for you." The broker lets this thought sink in and continues: "What I am primarily interested in is working with you when interesting opportunities develop - ideas we understand and are watching   closely, situations that you and your friend and I have that provide the same objective - to help you build your capital."

After a prospect admits that a life insurance agent has a better policy than the friend's coverage, the response could be: "I'm sure your friend would want you to do what's best for you, Ramesh. If he didn't feel this way, then he's not such a good friend after all. Now, let's do what we both know is in your family's best interest."

After a prospect admits that a life insurance agent has a better policy than the friend's coverage, the response could be: "I'm sure your friend would want you to do what's best for you, Ramesh. If he didn't feel this way, then he's not such a good friend after all. Now, let's do what we both know is in your family's best interest."

"I want to shop around"

When a prospect tells me this, I ask what other car(s) he has in mind. No matter what make, he says – Ford, Baleno, Lancer, Camri, you name it – I have a file on it. Let's say he says Lancer (it could be any make). Well, for years, I've saved all the newspaper and magazine articles on every automaker–all the articles telling about brakes not working, transmissions falling out, and so on.

The poor guy has to sit in my office and red pages and pages of problems that Lancer owners have had. Now am I doing anything that's not ethical? The way I see it, it's no different from a trial attorney pleading a case. When I finally re-enter the room, the prospect's face is as white as a sheet, and I say: "What do you think, Farooq, do you want to see three more files I have on Lancer?" Then I put the order pad in front of him and say, "Here, okay this. I'm probably saving your life!" It's amazing how meekly the prospect signs.

Of course, all salespeople can use this technique, no matter what you sell. Naturally, you have to do your homework and start a file on your competition. One easy way to get some negative information on a competitor is to call your local Associations and ask if it has a complaint file on XYZ Company. Be sure to say that you're considering doing business with XYZ Company. If they send you a long file of complaints, you can show it to your customers. If you dig, you're bound to come up with some negative facts about any company. If you can't, then that's the company you ought to see about a job.

In the selling business, it's common for people to shop around until they get what they believe is the best deal. So frequently, after you have spent an hour making a sales presentation and quoted a price on your product or service, the prospect will tell you, "I have a better offer."

Many salespeople start a shouting match with a buyer at this point. "This is not possible.. You can't beat this deal," they scream. This only scares the prospect away. What's more, you may end up challenging the prospect to prove he has a better offer. If you let him leave, you might prove your point, but you'll never see him again. It would cost him too much face to come back and admit he was wrong.

Sales people selling all types of products and services have come up against a bad salesperson, a low-ball con-artist, who quotes prices they know they can't sell at. BEWARE OF UNSCRUPULOUS SALESPEOPLE. They'll cost you time, lost sales, and frustration. These low-ball crooks hope the customer will come back after shopping around, unable to beat their price, and then they cop a plea. Their price, of course, did not include certain items, and the final price is always higher.

Now here's how Virender Singh would handle this kind of character. I would calmly say, "I think somebody has made a mistake. Don't tell me the salesman's name, but what dealership did he work for?" He says, "ABC Dealership." Then I continue, "Here's what I'm going to do for you, Sir, I'm going to prove to you that my deal was so fantastic, you're not going to believe it. What's more, I'm going to save you a lot of time by doing your shopping for you."

At this point, I call ABC Dealership and hand the telephone receiver to the prospect so he could hear it ringing. "Good afternoon, ABC," he hears.

I take the receiver from him and say, "Now, this is the place where you got that price, right?" After he acknowledges I called the right dealership, I ask to speak to a salesman.

"Sir, I bought a car three days ago from a dealer in town, and when I went to pick it up this morning, the salesman claims he made a five thousand rupees mistake. I am going to tell you what I want, and if you can give me your best deal, if it beats the one I have, I'll come right over and buy a car from you. But if your price is a single paisa more than what you tell me on the telephone, I am going to walk out. Is that fair?"

If the salesman tells me to come in or asks for my phone number, I reply, "No I only want you to give me a price, and if it's better than the one I have, my wife and I will be in this afternoon."

Almost always, the salesman will resist quoting a figure on the phone, but with persistence, he'll give a quote. In these situations, I know I've made such a low quote that nobody is going to beat it. Finally, the salesman quotes Rs. 6 lakhs. My quote was Rs. 5.8 lakhs and I whisper his figure to my prospect, who had been given a low-ball quote of Rs.5.6 lakhs from an ABC salesperson. Would you please repeat that number to my wife?" I ask, and I hand the phone receiver to the prospect.

"Six lakh rupees," he says, and I take the receiver away to speak to the salesman.

"Thank you very much," I say and hang up. Then I turn to my customer and tell him, "See, what did I tell you?" I put my pen in his hand and put it on the order. "Okay this for me", I say matter of fact.

Now and then a prospect will pull out a publication showing what appears to beat my deal. "Hey, look at this, Virender. It says right here," he says, pointing to a figure, "that I can buy it for rupees twenty thousand less than your quote."
He thinks he's going to shock me, but I simply tell him the price he sees can't be bought. It might not include the same options or dealer charges, I tell him, or it might be a bait-and-switch. That's a technique where the published price is very low, but when you ask for that model, the last one's always been sold, and they try to move you up to a more expensive one.
But after I've said all this, I don't ask the prospect to take it on faith. I use the same approach I explained before, calling the dealer and asking for a quote. I don't tell him I've seen his published price, just that I want his best price for this particular model with these particular options, all costs included.
It never fails. I always beat their price. Then I turn to the prospect.
"Put your okay right here," I'd tell him.
He accepts and okays it as I have beaten the real price of the competitor.

Now that you know, how to handle objections, it is important to move on to Supporting statements, as covered in the next chapter.

Chapter 10

SUPPORTING (S)
How to Reassure and Introduce Benefits?

In any situation demanding persuasion or communication between two persons there comes a phase when the person being pursued does make a favourable remark At this stage it is important to know the skills of how to support this favourable situation and to build on it for achieving agreement or acceptance. All successful people learn to follow the behavioural science approach to making supporting statements. This is done by:

(a) Reinforcement, where you rephrase a positive statement. It serves to reassure and reconfirm the point being made by the other person/customer.

(b) Introduction to an appropriate benefit by building on the favourable remark and elaborate the advantages to be derived from the acceptance of your idea / product.

Use of Supporting Statements
Supporting statements can be used to do the following:

1. Introduce a feature of an idea/product or a benefit to the other person/customer in the most logical way, from the other's point of view.
2. Capitalize/Voice the fact that you have a solution to the other person's problems.
3. Develop other person's agreement with your point of view.
4. Make a particular benefit or problem seem more important to the other person/customer.
5. Channelise a discussion towards your idea/product by giving your transitional phrases.

6. Help to control a discussion.
7. Allow bringing out only that idea/product information which is relevant.
8. Show your genuine interest in the other person.
9. Avoid disagreements.
10. Show that you are trying to solve things in a rational way.
11. Facilitate the prospect to reach conclusions that you would like him to develop on his own.
12. Maintain a conversational tone that helps the flow of valid information.

It can also be used to:
13. Digress onto a related topic.
14. Show friendliness.

Indicate that you have evidence to support what the other person has said. Usually Supporting Statements start in the following manner:

1. "Right, Mr. Sharma, for this reason we have..."
2. "Yes, and here is where..."
3. "That's true, so what you need is..."
4. "Absolutely right, therefore..."
5. "I agree with you, what you need is..."
6. "Rahul is important to you, and that is why..."
7. "I couldn't agree with you more; we can give you this..."
8. "That makes good sense. We feel the same way I can assure you of that..."

Therefore, you can say supporting statements are related to other (EPS) phases most often as a sequence to probing statements being used to uncover information that you can relate favourably with your idea/product. Also supporting statements help to introduce important benefits that you feel must be accepted, shown or provided before you can appropriately make a Closing Statement.

The next phase after supporting is proving which is covered in the next chapter.

Chapter 11

PROVING (P)
How to Prove and Expand Benefits?

During your communication with the other person there will be phases during the conversation when you will need to use statements for proving a point relevant to getting a "Yes". It is interesting that even in such an obvious stage, we can aim at getting maximum benefit. and making an impact. The following sequence is essential. However, its effectiveness is completely lost if one does not imbibe this sequence and learn it as a skill.

The sequence for making a proving statement is as follows:
1. **Restate the benefit** or the point to be proved before you prove it.
2. **Prove the benefit** or point by providing additional information, illustration, demonstration, example and/or data to achieve conviction.
3. **Expand the benefit:** This can be done by relating your information to the customer's situation. Show how his situation is similar to that of the proving source, explain the relevance of the information you have given and state the conclusion that you wish to make.

Interestingly, most people do not cover point (1) and (3) and so they are not able to get the full benefit of having the proof available to achieve acceptance. Therefore, disciplining oneself to following the above three step sequence during this phase is the hallmark of all skilled people who manage to achieve acceptance to their ideas/products in the shortest possible time.

Use of Proving Statements

Proving statements are designed to do the following:
1. Use available evidence to support what your idea / product will do.
2. Provide a before-and-after framework for any demonstration that you make.

3. Prove effectively any point that you wish to make (in addition to the fact that a special benefit will accrue to the prospect from the use of your idea / product).
4. Increase confidence in what you say.
5. Allow you to introduce references without name-dropping.
6. Overcome any doubt, scepticism, uncertainty or lack of credibility.

It can also be used to:

7. Prevent objections from ever coming up and remove suspicions arising from market rumours etc..
8. Provide a framework for the introduction of technical backup material or reports.
9. Show that you meet the standard that is expected of you before a decision is made.
10. Prove the existence of the problem, need or reason for dissatisfaction (in addition to the fact that the benefit will occur).

Proving statements are used whenever the prospect is aware of the benefit that you are discussing but is uncertain that you or your idea/product can infact provide this benefit. In relation to other EPS phases proving statements can be used to answer an easy objection or prove the benefit to help get a willing "Yes".

Some sample openings for making Proving statements are given below:

1. "We can do that very thing..."
2. "If you are concerned about the standards, let me show you..."
3. "I'm glad you brought up the subject..."
4. "Let me explain further how we..."
5. "What you're asking in effect is whether we can demonstrate..."
6. "I can see why you'd be interested in..."
7. "That's a very useful suggestion to look into..."

Some ways of expanding the benefits are as follows:

1. "If you went ahead with this..."
2. "This means you could be doing a better job than you are..."
3. "This will satisfy you by..."
4. "This illustrates what I said earlier, that you..."
5. "You will find that..."
6. "Going one step further, you will find..."

The skill to share proving statements as explained in this chapter can considerably improve your effectiveness in persuasion.

Now that you would have proved your point, the last step to getting a Yes is Closing. This is the most important step and is discussed in detail in the next chapter.

Chapter 12

CLOSING (C)

How to get an Agreement through a variety of Proven Techniques?

You have successfully closed a conversation when you have received your "Yes" from the other person. The technique of Closing means asking the other person a question, the positive answer to which helps to close the conversation by mutual acceptance of the proposition. There are eleven closing techniques that one can learn. And that can result in getting a 'yes' more easily, with greater appreciation and a better established goodwill from the other person. These closes are going to demand that you actually go through the hard-headed process of learning them. You will find, as you explore the domain of closing, especially in some advanced closes, the words themselves become very critical. But let's begin, by understanding the basic close.

But before that, some key questions.
☞ How many times should one take "no" for an answer before you accept it.? Once, twice or more. Now, here is an interesting truth. In a survey of 100 people, who earned top salaries, an interesting statistic came to light. These big time professionals, who were also infact, the greatest of closers; averaged their close on their fifth closing attempt. Which means, they encountered a "no" more than 4 times before they got a "Yes". When we find that the average person knows two closes and uses one, is there any question why this person stays average? We have so many ineffective persuaders in society.
☞ When do you start closing? The answer is - the minute you open your mouth. Because the whole inter-personal communication process is nothing but one big CLOSE.
☞ When do you close? I am a professional trainer, and have trained many people and I must, in complete honesty, tell you that I cannot tell you

when to close. Every person who is a great achiever has something we call a Closing instinct. You do not have to tell him when. He knows when. I can't tell you when. What I can tell you is, how to learn this. There is only one way in this world you will ever learn when to close, and that's by closing too soon and too often. If you keep on doing what you've been doing, closing too late and too seldom, you'll never learn to close. You learn to close by closing too soon and too often and in this way you develop a closing instinct.

Now let's talk about the basic close.

1. The "Simple Question" Close

This is the most fundamental of all closing methods and is always used by every professional. It's called the Simple Question close, and I am sure that anyone who is successful at persuasion, is using it because you can't succeed without it. In the Simple Question Close you begin by asking a question, the answer to the question, you fill on your contract/agreement/closing form. You don't ask, "Well, shall we go ahead?"

Now, what kind of question do you ask?
Obviously, to begin with: "What is your correct full name?" You fill it out. "Your correct mailing address/shipping address/delivery address?"

Now, you realize that as long as he doesn't stop you, he's bought! That's right! You assume he has bought. All you do is fill out the form. You just ask him one question after another until you have filled out the whole form. You have the whole thing now filled out.

What do you say when you get to the bottom? Not "sign it!" What's wrong with this word sign? What have you been told about signing things? You have been told 'read it', 'be careful', 'beware'. All your life you have heard people say, 'Don't sign anything'. The great persuaders today do it very simply - they just swing it around, hand the pen to the other person and say, "Would you okay this for me, please." It is strange, they won't sign it but they will okay it!

Now, in the next few lines, I am going to share with you some of the most important instructions in the field of closing. If you ever want to be a closer, these are the things you must remember because they are most fundamental. First of all, one must understand what a closing question is? Let me define it. A closing question is any question you ask the answer to which confirms the fact that your prospect is committed. 'What is your complete name?' 'What is your mailing address?' or any other fields in your closing form. These are closing questions. Now, the critical instruction whenever you ask a closing question is SHUT UP! Yes, Just Shut up! Remember this always - THE FIRST MAN THAT TALKS LOSES.

Many years ago, Mr Douglas Edwards, the father of closing techniques was training a major corporation. He was running a training class in New York City - a whole series of them, and he got to this point in the training and, for some reason, just before he got to this point the President of the Corporation came walking into the back of the room. He elaborated the "SHUT UP" point and the President jumped up into the air, got up, turned around and walked right out of the room. The next week Douglas was running another session and just about the same time (he must have got hold of a schedule), the President walked back into the room.

When the class had settled down, he said 'Douglas, do you mind if I say something?' Douglas said, 'Of course not, come on up.' So he came up. He said, 'You know when I was in this class room last week, I heard this for the first time, it amused me and I decided to try it. Within the past few days, one of the top organisations in America has been in here trying to lease us a product that will cost us a million dollars a year'. And he said, 'You know, these must be real good persuaders because one of them asked me a closing question, and he shut up, and Douglas, so did I! By my watch there wasn't a sound in that room for twenty minutes. He said, 'You know what happened? I bought'.

This is critical. You see if you shut up, only one of two things can happen:
(i)   The other person goes along with you, or
(ii) gives you a reason for not going along. As a skilled person you can catch either one. But what happens to you, usually? - There is three quick seconds of silence and you get itchy. Now you have to add something. And you open your big mouth and the other person is off the hook. There is no pressure that will remotely approach the pressure of silence. There is one person who got a million dollars a year order for sitting there for twenty minutes. Twenty minutes. That feels like an eternity. I submit that these two words - SHUT UP - are the most important words you will learn as an Effective persuasion skill.

2. The "Alternative Choice" Close

Now there are all kinds of alternative choices; you always give the other person a choice - You give them a choice of buying this, buying that, buying this way or buying that way. It is important that you give the choices in the correct way:

"You want your premiums monthly or annually?" This doesn't say, 'Are you going to pay the premiums monthly or annually?' You assume they are going to pay them, the only question is how. The only word of objection to is "pay." Now what's another choice: Cash or Credit Card? Do you prefer the deluxe or standard? Which do you prefer, the white or the grey? Always start them out with this phrase, 'which do you prefer?'

3. The "Ben Franklin" Close

Some of you might be familiar with the Ben Franklin close. It is one of the most popular closes. It explores something called the "Ben Franklin Balance Sheet". This is one of those closes which is a simple one to handle complex situations. You are going to have to learn the words and have them right. The words here are critical. This close is definitely great and here's the way it works. You can use this on the person who is just indecisive; you can't really tell him; you can get no specific reason out of him; he just won't jell down. And you want to jell him hard!

You start with what we call a story close, and it goes this way.
"As you know, Americans have long considered Benjamin Franklin one of our wisest men. Whenever old Ben found himself in a situation such as you are in today, he felt pretty much as you do about it. If it was the right thing to do, he wanted to be sure and did it. If it was the wrong thing, he wanted to be sure and avoid it. Isn't that about the way you feel? Here's what old Ben used to do. He would take a sheet of plain white paper (now you take a sheet of plain white paper) and he would draw a line down the middle (and you draw a line down the middle). On this side he wrote "yes" (pointing to the left hand column) and on the other side wrote "no" (putting that on the top of the right hand column). And then here (pointing to yes) he would list all the reasons favouring his decision and here (pointing to no) the reasons against it. When he was through he simply counted the numbers in each column and his decision was made for him. Why don't we try it and see what happens? Now you swing the paper around, put it in front of him, hand him your pen and say, Let's see how many reasons we can think of favouring your decision today." And now you give him all the help in the world. How about this, how about that, don't you think that this is a good point and so on. You can plug this to 20 or more. And then when you get to the no area you just say, "Now let's see how many reasons you can think of against it" and you keep quiet. I have yet to see more than 4 on the no side.

Do you realize what's happening to this prospect's mind? You start on the yeses, and he can't switch back to no, to think of more than four, and then all you do, is to start counting the yeses - "one, two, three, four... twenty, twenty-one, twenty-two.... Okay, that's twenty-four on this side, let's see what have we got on this side - One, two, three. Well, the answer is pretty obvious, isn't it it."

4. **The next close is an inversion of the Ben Franklin Balance Sheet.** This, however, is oral. Again to be used, on a procrastinating person who can't quite give a reason for dallying alone, but just isn't going. Now this is what we call a negative yes close. By this I mean in this close we allow him to say no, but every time he says "no"he means yes. Now you always start it this way:

"Just to clarify my thinking (you're the idiot, he never is), what is it that isn't quite clear to you? Is it the integrity of (and here you name your Company)."
'No', he says.
"Is it my personal integrity?"
"No".
You see, this 'no' means 'yes'. And you now start summarizing all of the facets of your presentation, one question at a time by asking him, "Is it this?"/ "Is it that?".Now, each time you ask 'is it' and he says 'no', you've got a 'yes', haven't you?

5. **The "Similar Situation" Close**
This is the old favourite of the Insurance Industry. The strange thing is that this is the only Industry I know of that uses it and they are losing it? This is the make them sob close. And this applies to almost any situation I know of. How many times in your life have you had an insurance salesman start closing as follows:

You know, it was just a couple of weeks ago I was sitting in a home, with a, young couple just like you sitting in there with me. I was trying to make a presentation to this young couple, trying to point out to them how critical insurance was to their very lives. They had a little daughter about 3-1/2 or 4 years old, short hair, real cute, but kind of eccentric. First thing she did was climb in her father's lap, and he shoves her off, and then she climbs in her mother's lap, and she shoves her off - next thing I knew she was climbing into my lap, and there I was trying to sell insurance to her parents and I couldn't shove her off. Her mother finally came to my rescue. She picked this little girl up and spanked her little behind, and she went crying out of the room. Well, I didn't get these people to take a decision that night. You know, just yesterday morning I picked up the paper and cried. Because that mother and father had just been killed in an automobile accident, and I'm haunted by it, not because of the mother and father but all I can think of is that child. That child who was so desperate for affection that she crawled into the lap of a stranger. I feel sorry and consider it my failure that I could not get them to make the right decision. I don't want to make that mistake again with you.

Now just as effective, is a similar situation in which you define someone else's happiness or success because he did similar to what you are suggesting. There is no reason why any person cannot tell a story about someone who decided to do what is being suggested and achieved a happy result that was rather unexpected. You see what you do is to put them in somebody else's place, so that they imagine that it's them.

But why should this be limited to insurance? This can be used in day to day situations to get agreement and acceptance. By telling stories about somebody who made the right decision, I look good because he made that decision. It assures you that you can make this decision and look fine too. It is similar to story telling. We've lost story telling in getting a yes, but people love stories.

6. The "Call Back" Close

A person says to you, "I want more time to review this" and you say, alright. Then you go and a week or so later you come back and the first words you say are "Well, did you think it over" and he says "Yes / No". This is the wrong way to handle the situation.

Now its important to learn how to handle "I'll think it over". I'm going to tell you how to catch it so that whenever he says "I'll think it over" instead of saying "Oh, Hell" you'll say "Great". But before we get to that, I want to share an idea. The only thing you can do to save a call back situation is when you walk in, to see this person that you have to call back on for a decision, you start out by saying, "I'm very sorry but the last time I was here, there was something I forgot to tell you - I think it's important". Now tell him something new. After you have told him something new, you go on by saying "Let me just review briefly the things we talked about the last time." Now you give him the whole presentation all over again. I mean it - the whole presentation, the only difference being, that this time you occasionally begin your sentence with – 'As you remember /you will recall /we said that / we agreed on that'. But give him the whole presentation and go into the normal closing sequence and don't ever ask him if he thought it over, instead ask a relevant closing question.

7. The "Lost Case" Close

For endless years trainers have stood on platforms and have trained using the traditional "lost case" close. It was theoretically perfect - only one problem, it didn't work. Lets talk about it because it is one of those things that are perfect theoretically, but require a practical touch.

One time I had a friend who was a whole lot smarter than I was. He took this lost case close and he put a switch into it that made it work. Old hat-and it worked, with the switch. This is the close to use when you've lost it this to be used when everything else you've tried has failed. The other person is red in the face, his fists clenched or else you have run out of steam and quit. Do this. Pack up, then as you get to the door, stop, hesitate, turn around (this is still old stuff) and you say, 'Pardon me, I wonder if you would help me for a moment' - (old stuff, old theory, didn't work, but here comes the switch) 'Before I go on, (this is part of the close) may I apologise to you for being so inept a communicator. You see, if I had been able to make you feel the way I feel about this home I am recommending, you would have owned it now. Your children would be planning to play in this backyard, out of the dirt, your wife would have been anticipating this wonderful kitchen but your children aren't going to have this yard to play in, your wife is going to keep on working in that old kitchen and cleaning that old home and I want you to know that I know that it's all my fault; and I'm truly sorry.' (That's the switch? Now we go back to old hat) 'As you can see, I have to earn my living this way. Just so I don't make the same mistake again, would you mind telling me what I did that was wrong?'

Now everything about this is old hat except the apology. Did you ever apologise for not getting a yes? Let me tell you, if there is a need for your proposal and the prospect has the financial capacity, if they didn't agree, it is your fault, nobody else's. Don't go around blaming the other person; this is the fault of inept communicators.. If there is a need or desire, if the prospect qualifies and if they don't agree, it's your fault, not theirs, and you ought to apologise. Also by the way, it works.

But when you use this apology, you better mean it. If you are at all cute about it, they will toss you out on your ear. But if, when you apologise to them for being an inept communicator you mean it, and you should mean it, if you apologise with sincerity, you will find this lost case close gets you a Yes.

8. The "Sharp Angle" Close

This one you save for that situation when someone asks you about your proposal in this way - 'Can it do this, can it do that, will it do this for me, will it do that for me?'

How do you sharp angle instead of your simply telling for sure it'll do it. You sharp angle by saying "Do you want it if it does?" When the other person agrees to want it if it does, you have got the acceptance upon providing proof. But if you were to simply go ahead and prove that it does, you have no confirmation and no acceptance. This is sharp angling.

Now I'm going to tell you about the two most important Closes: Closing on "a final objection" and "I'll think it over". These two closes are a top combination because if you master these two closes, your persuasion skills will improve perceptibly and so will your happiness and success in life.

9. The "Final Objection" Close

Let me set the scene for you. Normally, when you reach for your first close a person seldom says No. Normally he gives you an objection. Then you answer the objection. Now you get involved in this death knell of the persuader: can he think of more objections than you can answer or can you answer more than he can think of? As fast as you kill one, he pops another. Now would you like to have a method of taking the first objection that you hear and making it the last one? Alright, here's how you do it. I'm going to give you a formula first and then I'll go back and explain the formula.

1. Hear him out.
2. Emphasize to him the importance of his objection.
3. Confirm the objection.
4. Question it.
5. Answer it.
6. Confirm the answer.
7. Close it.

Here's what happens, when he tries to explain this to you. One of these things happens:

1. He does explain it, now he's hooked on it even further, isn't he? (Of course, I'm assuming you can answer the objection. If you can't, you're in real trouble.) He actually re-explains it, and hooks himself on it, harder.
2. In the process of trying to explain it, he touches on the real objection.
3. In the process of explaining it, it looks stupid even to him. Endless times I've had people trying to explain one of these things to me and all of a sudden look at me and say, "Oh Hell" because it didn't even make sense to him anymore but he has told me that this is the only thing in the way.

Where does he go from here? Well, let's assume he reconfirms himself to this objection. Now what do you do to answer him. After you have answered it, you confirm it by saying 'Now that completely settles that, doesn't it?' Where does he go? He has told you this was the only thing standing between you and him. Now that this stands answered you can get your 'yes'.

10. Closing on "I'll think it over"

Tell you what. I'm just not the kind of person who likes to make snap judgements. You let me sleep on this overnight, we'll probably go along with you but I just hate to rush. I can't make a decision right now but let me think it over.

110

You've heard this, haven't you? When a person says to you 'I'll think it over', You say to him, 'That's fine. Obviously you wouldn't take your time thinking it over unless you were really interested, would you. I'm sure you're not telling me this just to get rid of me. So may I assume you will give it a very careful consideration.' He thinks you're going to let him go. He thinks, 'Great, this guy is going to let me go'. So he agrees all the way. He'll give it very careful consideration.

'Just to make my thinking, clearer what phase of this proposal is it that you want to think over? Is it the integrity of (name your firm), is it my..........?' What am I doing to him? We are summarily closing him. What's going to happen to him? We're going to say is it this, no, is it that - no, is it that, no. All of a sudden he's going to realize what is happening and he's going to say 'Yes, that's it'. Now what've you got? You've got a final objection. Now close on the final objection and you tell me where he goes.

You see, the problem with 'I'll think it over' is very simple - there's nothing to get your teeth into. What you have to do is to take "I'll think it over," and reduce it to a specific objection because you can handle an objection, you can't handle something intangible.

Now in this, "I'll think it over" close, there is one point where, if you stop for breath you will blow the whole bit. Think you can find that point?

'What phase of the proposal is it, that you want to think over.' You see, if you say 'What phase of the proposal is it that you want to think over.' He says, "the whole thing." Then you are in trouble.. You've got to get him to that first "is it..........?" without stopping for breath. Once you get into that first 'Is it' you are on your way to getting 'yes' and that's the technique to be used for 'I'll think it over'. Learn to use it because I guarantee that if you can use it with skill when they say 'I'll think it over', you will feel confident that you can now use your skills to get a "yes".

11. The "Question" Close

Finally, I'm going to try and lead you to cut your lost opportunities. I'm going to point out a closing opportunity that is laid in our lap five to ten times a day, everyday of our lives, and most of us muff it. You would have muffed more opportunities to close than you can possibly imagine. I'm going to prove it to you now - simply because most people talk too much.

Did you ever have anyone say to you, for example, 'Can I get it in green?' What do you say, 'Yes, you can get it in green'. Question closing demands that you say, 'do you want it in green?' Now that he says, 'Yes' he's agreed. How many of these opportunities have you faced every day of your life? How many times a day do people ask you simple questions like these and you sit there and open your mouth and tell them, 'Yes, yes, we can do it." This is something you cannot ignore, and if you will just listen to the other person's needs today, in theprocess of getting a yes, I bet you can find many such opportunities to get acceptance that otherwise, you would have missed.

I've tried to provide you with the single most essential persuasion skill you need - the skill of CLOSING. With this skill, you can enhance your effectiveness manifold. Read this chapter periodically to sharpen these techniques. Try them out in your day-to-day conversation. Keep a tally on how many times did you try to close before you got acceptance. Try and count how many closing techniques have you started using in your daily life. If you can increase the number gradually, by repetitive study you will become more and more proficient. Do not think that one reading will equip you to use these techniques. Practice does make perfect. You will need to practise these techniques to become skilled. But they are satisfying and a lot of fun.So go ahead, use them, develop them, expand them and go and get acceptances and commitments with a feeling of a well prepared and skilled individual. Enjoy the success that awaits you. Yes!

Chapter 13

CHECKLIST OF GOLDEN RULES ON EFFECTIVE PERSUASION SKILLS (EPS)

How the acronym 'OPOSPC' can Change Your Life for the Better

Now that you have learnt about the six skills of Effective Persuasion, it is important that you remember them. The acronym OPOSPC is all that you need to memorize. Each alphabet of the acronym represents an important skill as follows:

Opening Statement,

Probing,

Objections handling,

Supporting statements,

Proving statements,

Closing

The Golden Rules you need to keep in mind at every skill stage are as follows:

Opening Statement

Always open your conversation starting with what you feel would be of interest to the other person. Do not start with what you want.

Probing

1. Probe non-directly when you want to discuss things that the other person feels are important.
2. Probe directly when you want to discuss things that you feel are important.

Objection Handling

1. All objections must be responded to by restating the objection to the other person in question form. This is essential in order to avoid any mis-communication or misunderstanding. It helps to fully understand the real objection and win empathy as well.
2. Easy objections should be answered directly, offering proof in your response.
3. Difficult objections should be handled by emphasizing other relevant benefits so as to minimize the genuine disadvantages.

Supporting Statements

1. Always offer agreement or reinforcement to the other person's favourable remark. Do not let it go unacknowledged or taken for granted.
2. Introduce a supporting benefit relevant to the other person.

Proving Statement

1. Always restate the benefits of your proposal or idea.
2. Prove it by giving proof through factual data or examples.
3. Expand it by elaborating other related benefits.

Closing

1. You must assume that the acceptance/commitment from the other person already exists. It is strange but true that what you think tends to happen, so you must think that the other person will agree.
2. You must summarize important benefits to the other person.
3. You must ask for explicit acceptance of your proposal/idea by making a statement or asking a question such that the answer does not provide for No as a possible response. This is possible by using the various closing techniques mentioned earlier - such as, Alternate choice.
4. After making a closing statement or asking a closing question. WAIT. Let the other person answer. The power of silence is very strong. Do not get tempted to further reinforce your closing statement or question, as this is a major blunder which the uninitiated commit.
5. Based on your closing statement or question there will either be an acceptance or agreement to your proposal / idea or another objection. If there is an objection then handle the objection, support your point, prove it and ask for acceptance (close) again.

This model of Effective Persuasion Skills (EPS) consisting of six skills as reflected by the acronym "OPOSPC" will show you the way to a ready YES when you would otherwise be stuck with a NO.

Most people do not know how to handle a No or a rejection or an objection other than to get angry and frustrated. Now by using the six basic skills model of OPOSPC you can remain cool and get acceptance and agreement on any proposal or idea which has real merit and benefits. All successful people who can get a YES to their ideas or proposals use this in one way or the other, partly or fully. You are now equipped with this powerful model that will show you the way from blind alleys and road blocks in conversations to smooth sails, overcoming the negative with skill, ease and confidence.

Let us now summarise this in the final chapter.

Chapter 14

SUMMARY

How Can You be Many Times More Effective as an Individual Using EPS

Once you begin using the EPS model of OPOSPC, as a natural outcome, your effectiveness to persuade people in an agreeable and pleasant manner will become manifold. From now on do the following:

1. Always plan on making an 'opening statement' which reflects the interest of the other person whether your relative, friend, co-worker, boss, customer or who ever. Think for a few moments before presenting your proposal or idea. To initiate it, keep in mind the interest or benefit that the other person would have in the subject.

2. Always 'probe' to understand the views of the other person instead of assuming/guessing them. They will be pleasantly happy to realize that you are giving consideration and importance to their concerns.

3. Handle 'objections' with deeper understanding by rephrasing the objections in question form. This is a must to come on the same wavelength and fully understand what the actual objections are.
    Having understood the real objections in detail, go ahead and answer them giving facts and proof as required.

4. Support your proposal/idea and don't assume that it requires no elaboration. For generating better understanding and agreement supporting the customer's positive statement by agreeing with it is an important step that is often over-looked.

5. Use 'proving statements' to provide proof of your proposal/idea in definitive terms through facts and examples.

6. Use 'Closing Techniques' to explicitly ask for acceptance all the time assuming that the other person will be in agreement. Summarize all the benefits of your proposal/idea so that acceptance to your closing

statement or question is easily and voluntarily forthcoming. Normally, people know of one or two or maximum three closing methods but now you have been made aware of 12 closing method to get acceptance of your proposal/idea. This should help you manifold in your day to day interaction.

Please review these closing techniques, as well as the six skills of EPS regularly, again and again, till they become second nature to your approach. Present your proposals/ideas to get a YES with confidence, ease and appreciation from the other person. You are now on the path to being many times more effective in your everyday interactions with other people - not only to get their acceptance and agreement but to also get their respect, affection and appreciation. This is because by practicing this unique approach you would have made a sincere effort to understand them in an in-depth manner and handled their objections skillfully as well.

This sums up **The Art of Getting People to Say YES.** The more you practise and implement EPS the more successful and happy you will be in your ability to persuade other people to say YES in an agreeable and pleasant manner. Use this model many times a day to be many times more effective day after day Enjoy your new life as an effective and likeable persuader who can always get a YES to all ideas and proposals you sincerely believe in.

Other Books by WVPD (Wisdom Village Publications Division)

World acclaimed book,
When You Are Sinking Become A Submarine

Available in Hindi as
ऐसा पाल तानें कि आँधी ऊर्जा बने

Rs. 245/- 184p ISBN 81-8328-052-8

Rs. 150/- 186p ISBN 81-906555-3-8

It's the first time I've ever read anything like it, and I imagine it's the best introduction. I really enjoy how he looks at people, and I'm learning a lot... I tell people, don't go with Eckhart Tolle just because Oprah says you should. Go with someone who does it because they honestly have something interesting to say."

- Carolyn Marcille (Barnes & Noble, New York, USA)

Success Sutras For The 21st Century: A Trilogy Of Wisdom

Rs. 290/- (Hard Cover in a Box) ISBN 81-90655-4-5 / Rs. 65/- each (Paperback)

Pavan Choudary's passion for dwelling deep into the questions one feels remain unanswered, has ensured him a place amongst the foremost thinkers of the world. **- The Times of India**

Each book in this collection of mini books has great depth...their is great insight on political sharpness, social gain and spiritual intelligence - to aid the ambitious soul. **- The Hindustan Times**

Pavan Choudary is also the author of **The RX Factor**-A Path Breaking Business Book.
For more details, testimonials, Indian & International press coverage, visit **www.starcoach.co.in**

Dr. Anand P.Verma
Healing In Your Hands
Rs. 250/- 222p ISBN978-81-906555-1-4

FORTHCOMING Books by WVPD

To book your orders: E-mail: wisdomvillageindia@gmail.com or call +91 9811514287